EL DORADO IN THE MARSHES

EL DORADO IN THE MARSHES

Gold, Slaves and Souls between the Andes and the Amazon

MASSIMO LIVI BACCI

TRANSLATED BY CARL IPSEN

polity

This English edition © Polity Press, 2010

Polity Press
65 Bridge Street
Cambridge CB2 1UR, UK

Polity Press
350 Main Street
Malden, MA 02148, USA

ISBN-13: 978-0-7456-4552-0 (hardback)
ISBN-13: 978-0-7456-4553-7 (paperback)

A catalogue record for this book is available from the British Library.

Typeset in 10.75 on 14 pt Adobe Janson
by Servis Filmsetting Ltd, Stockport, Cheshire
Printed and bound in Great Britain by MPG Books Limted, Bodmin, Cornwall

The publisher has used its best endeavours to ensure that the URLs for external websites referred to in this book are correct and active at the time of going to press. However, the publisher has no responsibility for the websites and can make no guarantee that a site will remain live or that the content is or will remain appropriate.

Every effort has been made to trace all copyright holders, but if any have been inadvertently overlooked the publisher will be pleased to include any necessary credits in any subsequent reprint or edition.

For further information on Polity, visit our website: www.politybooks.com

The translation of this work has been funded by SEPS
SEGRETARIATO EUROPEO PER LE PUBBLICAZIONI
SCIENTIFICHE

Via Val d'Aposa 7 - 40123 Bologna - Italy
seps@seps.it - www.seps.it

CONTENTS

ILLUSTRATIONS

Plates

FIGURES AND TABLES

INTRODUCTION

Long ago I made a brief and unplanned stop in Bogotá. Not so brief, though, that I didn't manage to scramble to the top of Monserrate, the mountain that looms over the city and surrounding plateau. Today I like to think that I spied in the distance the edge of the high prairie, the *sabana*, where the myth of El Dorado was born in 1538, a myth that derived from the remarkable and accidental meeting of three adventurer-conquistadors: the hapless Sevillian lawyer Jiménez de Queseda, the German captain Nicolaus Federman, and the powerful friend of Francisco Pizarro, Sebastián de Benalcázar. That unexpected stopover also allowed me to quickly visit the Museo del Oro and its extraordinary collection of objects fashioned by the Chibcha goldsmiths whose advanced civilization was swept up in the hurricane of the Conquest. These rich objects, full of fantasy, were displayed – or perhaps more accurately lumped together – in a few narrow and well-guarded rooms of the Banco Nacional de Colombia. That visit, a short stopover in an odyssey of airports, retreated into the depths of memory. Many years later, it was the curiosity of Nicoletta, my wife, that took me to the Brazilian Pantanal, a vast region flooded for much of the year by the waters of the Paraguay river and its tributaries but dry when those waters retreat during the long arid months. A number of small ethnic groups inhabited these lands, surviving on hunting, fishing, and rudimentary agriculture; their mark on history is a faint one. There was seemingly no link between these two visits, separated by thousands of kilometers, the towering Andes Mountains, and thirty years of time. And yet a link did emerge, first in vague outline and then more precisely, as I conducted research on the demography of the American Indios in the Jesuit Archive in Rome (ARSI). For, as I discovered, in the late seventeenth century the spiritual followers of Saint Ignatius Loyola created a network of missions in the plains of the Mojos at the foot of the Andes, an area similar to the Brazilian Pantanal in that it is flooded by the waters of the upper Madeira river, a principal tributary of the Amazon. That network was second only (in terms of population, organization, and importance) to the thirty missions of Paraguay. The Spaniards explored this region relatively late, and it was long considered a mysterious province inhabited by a people possessing a wealth of gold and precious stones: an El Dorado, or Paititi, or Realm of the Grand Mojo, or land of the *Gran Noticia*. It was an El Dorado that beginning in the 1530s became an obsession for the conquistadors, inspiring them to cross the Andes and explore the unknown eastern forests in expeditions that were often disastrous and always disappointing. An elusive El Dorado that as the expeditions proceeded was always farther east, or farther south, or in any case beyond the horizon. The land of the Mojos – in what is today eastern Bolivia – was the farthest and latest goal of these expeditions. The Spaniards looked for gold, but they found a swamp. And so the link between those two visits emerged out of vague memories and so, unexpectedly, the idea to write this book.

Half a century after Columbus first crossed the Atlantic, his followers had acquired a basic knowledge of the shape of the American continent. The arrival of Columbus led to the exploration and settlement of the Greater and Lesser Antilles as well as much of the Caribbean coast including present-day Venezuela and Colombia. In 1513, Balboa crossed the Isthmus of Panama and came upon the "Mar del Sur," that is the Pacific Ocean. In 1520, Magellan rounded Cape Horn and so opened a sea passage between the two oceans. The expedition of Juan de Solís explored the Rio de la Plata and its estuary starting in 1515. Diego de Ordáz sailed up the Orinoco in 1531, and in 1540 Francisco de Orellana navigated the full length of the Amazon, from the slopes of the Andes to the open sea. The conquests of Mexico and Perú advanced European exploration and settlement in Meso-America and the Andes. Meanwhile Portuguese colonists were occupying strategic points on the coast of Brazil. Great pre-Colombian urban centers like Mexico, Quito, and Cuzco were converted into European cities, while new cities were founded that would become great metropolises in subsequent centuries: Havana, Santo Domingo, Bogotá, Lima, Santiago, and Buenos Aires. Already by 1550 there were several tens of thousands of colonists spread throughout the continent. Each year dozens of ships linked America and Europe, bringing adventurers and colonists, administrators and religious, merchants and artisans, but also microbes, seeds, plants, animals, and tools. Chronicles, reports, letters, and oral testimonies quickly spread news of the New World throughout Europe. The speed with which the entire continent was explored, subdued, and settled amazed the entire world, including the conquistadors themselves.

Why did the Conquest proceed so quickly? There are

of course a number of reasons. One of these was the great advances in navigation that made it possible to cross the oceans with relative ease and minimal risk and so establish intensive and constant traffic between the two continents. Equally important was the large technological and information gap between Europeans and the indigenous Americans, a relative advantage that allowed the one group to subdue the other in spite of a huge numeric disparity; it was a gap that owed more to organizational and logistic capability than to the possession of firearms, steel weapons, and horses. The Conquest was also the natural extension of the commercial and economic expansion that had led to the exploitation of the Atlantic islands and the African coast. In terms of human resources, Spain possessed a large class of *hidalgos* characterized by great ambition, but limited wealth, and raised in a warrior tradition that made them eager for adventure. The hope of finding rich lands and wealthy populations to subdue played a role as did the opportunity to convert those populations to the true religion. Of overwhelming importance on an individual level was of course the hope of getting rich, what Pietro Martire described as the "deadly hunger for gold." In the first phase of the Conquest, many of the invaders perished from drowning in the sea or a river, getting lost on a march or expedition, being killed in a battle with the natives or in a skirmish among rival factions, or succumbing to starvation and disease. Whole expeditions disappeared without leaving a trace. The greater the risk, the greater the wager, and so the greater the expectation of instant wealth. The myth of El Dorado was born of the desperate hope for riches and was a significant stimulus for adventures and explorations, many of which turned out to be vain leaps into the darkness. At the same time, an extraordinary combination of legend and fact contributed to its promulgation.

El Dorado in the Marshes traces the rise of this myth and

its demise as that trajectory relates to a population – the Mojos – who inhabited the vast plains of eastern Bolivia, an expanse that lies under water for many months of the year. Contact with Europeans was sporadic and difficult because of the special settlement characteristics of the Mojos and their great distance from the centers of colonization. For Europeans, the land of the Mojos was one of many associated with the myth of El Dorado, home of the mysterious and fabulously wealthy Grand Mojo. As it turned out, explorations gradually revealed that the inhabitants of the muddy plains were relatively backward and desperately poor, populations that because of their dispersion and low density lent themselves poorly to the usual sort of exploitation that allowed the Spaniards to enrich themselves, even when the Europeans failed to find gold, silver, or precious stones. They were, however, populations that managed to maintain themselves in a difficult environment thanks to an extraordinary ability to adapt; and for nearly a century that vitality persisted under the administration of the Jesuits. After the Jesuits were expelled, the corruption of secular clergy and civil administrators who replaced them, combined with late-nineteenth-century migration for the harvesting of rubber, led to a long and hard decline. Among the Mojos, as throughout the Americas, the Europeans brought about a revolution that was at once demographic, cultural, and economic.

Note

For much of this book I make no particular claim to originality, as the events narrated here are well known to Hispanists and the relevant documentation has been published over the past two centuries. In chapters IV and V, instead, I have used unpublished material from ARSI, in addition to generally known sources. Wherever possible I have let the actors and narrators speak for themselves, taking the necessary liberties to resolve linguistic-syntactic ambiguities that would have made a literal translation potentially incomprehensible to readers today.

I should like to thank Nicoletta Basilotta, librarian at the IHSI (Institutum Historicum Societatis Jesu), and Maria del Carmen Diez-Hoyo, director of the Biblioteca Hispánica of Madrid, for the help that they gave me at various stages in the project. Their kindness was only matched by their expertise.

I

A GOLD NUGGET LARGER THAN A SUCKLING
PIG; THE TREASURE OF ATAHUALLPA
ENRICHES 64 HORSEMEN, 138 FOOT
SOLDIERS, AND THE KING OF SPAIN; EL
DORADO, A VAIN CACIQUE COVERED IN
GOLD DUST WASHES OFF IN THE LAKE;
STORIES OF AMAZONS AND A GREEK
ARTILLERYMAN

In 1501, in the Cibao mountains not far from Santo Domingo, an Indio woman working for a Spanish prospector named Miguel Diaz made a stunning discovery. Near the Hayna river where she was sieving for gold, she found an enormous nugget – "like a great bread loaf from Alcalá" – that weighed 3,600 pesos (about 16 kilograms) of which only about 300 (according to expert miners) consisted of impurities. The nugget was taken to the city, weighed, displayed to the colonists (Las Casas saw it),[1] and guarded so that it could be shown to the king and queen in Spain. Miguel Diaz and his partner, Francisco de Garay, were paid the equivalent in gold (less the *"quinto"* owed to the crown). Gonzalo Fernández de Oviedo narrates that when the Indio brought the nugget to her masters:

> Overjoyed, they decided to dine on a nice fat suckling pig. One of them said "I have long wished I could dine on plates of gold. Since we could make many plates from this nugget, I want to eat off it." And so they did. On that valuable plate they ate the pig. And the whole pig fit on it since, as I said, it was so big.[2]

It was a jolly and tasty meal, though the nugget came to a bad end. In early July 1502 it left with the fleet of thirty ships (carrying about 600 people as well as 200,000 pesos of gold and other precious stones) taking the Governor Francisco de Bobadilla back to Spain. The fleet encountered a violent storm only ten leagues from the coast, and just seven or eight of the ships survived and made it back to Spain. Bobadilla, 500 others, and all the gold were lost in the deep. It is worth recalling that Bobadilla was the governor sent to Hispaniola two years before to arrest Columbus and his brothers, Bartolomé and Diego, who had been accused of misgovernment; he had sent them back in chains. Columbus was subsequently pardoned by the monarchs, though forbidden to return to Hispaniola, and left on his fourth voyage. On 29 June he took refuge in the bay of Puerto Hermosa in order to wait out the storms. Las Casas tells us that Columbus recommended to the governor that he not depart with his fleet because of the risks posed by the weather.[3] Bobadilla chose to ignore the warning, though that story really isn't part of our narrative.

The story of the huge nugget shows that the urgency of the search for gold (what Pietro Martire, a chronicler of the Conquest, called "the deadly hunger for gold"[4]) was fed by dramatic episodes like this one, episodes that, by force of

repetition and exaggeration, ratcheted up the feverish desire
for the precious mineral. Ovando came to the island in 1502
to replace Bobadilla as governor. He brought with him an
expedition of 2,500 souls many of whom became foolhardy
prospectors, venturing out into difficult territory with inad-
equate equipment, not enough food, and little knowledge.
Needless to say, many of these, including men of high rank
and with no experience at manual labor, perished. Up to
one-third of the native adults on the island were employed
in the search for gold (digging up the river deposits, sieving,
and washing). They found a great deal: the authorized (and
so taxed) casting sent back to Seville amounted to over 600
kilograms per year in the first decade of the century,[5] but the
real total was surely much higher. As the placers and veins
were exhausted and the indigenous population declined,
the gold flowing back to Spain slowed to a trickle and then
ceased altogether. The same thing happened in Cuba and
Puerto Rico and, later on, along the "Castilla de Oro" (the
Caribbean coast of what is today Costa Rica and Panama).

The legend of New World gold, which would never entirely
fade, reached its zenith in the 1530s. The horrible ransom
demanded by Pizarro – a fabulous amount of gold and silver
in exchange for the life of Atahuallpa, who had been taken
prisoner by the Spaniards at Cajamarca – sparked the wild
imagination of the conquistadors. The wretched Atahuallpa
promised – these are the words of Francisco de Xeres whom
Pizarro charged with writing and signing the account in July
1533 – "'I will give enough gold to fill a room twenty-two
feet long and seventeen wide, up to a white line which is half
way up the wall.' The height would be up to a man's stature
and a half [. . .] As for silver, he said he would fill the whole
chamber with it twice over. He undertook to do this in two
months." For weeks the Indios filed into Cajamarca carrying
on their shoulders precious gold and silver objects to fill the

ransom rooms up to the height a man can reach with his arm outstretched.[6] Devotional objects, dishes, bowls, platters, and urns taken from temples, sepulchers, and palaces arrived from throughout the empire. Precious loot came from as far away as Cuzco, 200 leagues (more than 1,000 kilometers) from Cajamarca. Three Spaniards were sent there with a local contingent to speed up the consignment that included 700 sheets of gold torn from the walls of a temple. Day after day for two months the objects accumulated to the amazement of the greedy Spaniards, until Atahuallpa's promise was fulfilled and Pizarro's betrayed. "Most of the gold consisted of panels like those from wooden trunks three or four palms in length and a palm or more in width; they had been torn off the walls of temples and had holes where nails had held them to the walls."[7]

Beginning on 13 May, 1533, an army of Indian artisans and laborers worked at nine furnaces to melt down the gold. It was cast in bars, weighed, marked, and shipped out; the job was completed by 25 July. In all there were 1,326,539 pesos of "good gold" (nearly 6,000 kilograms) and 26,000 pounds of silver (about 12,000 kilograms).[8] Oviedo believed that a large portion of the ransom gold never made it to the official casting; whatever the case, it was a huge amount. After compensation had been paid to the foundryman, the royal "*quinto*" was counted out and sent back to the King in Spain, together with the most beautiful objects that had not been melted down, under the guidance of Hernando Pizarro, Francisco's brother, who on his return enjoyed honors, privileges, and payment at the Spanish court. The *Santa Maria del Campo* docked in Seville on 9 January, 1534, carrying 463,000 pesos in gold bars for the monarch, in addition to:

> thirty-eight vases of gold and forty-eight of silver, among
> which there was an eagle of silver. In its body were fitted

two vases and two large pots, one of gold and the other of silver, each of which was capable of containing a cow cut into pieces. There were also two sacks of gold, each capable of holding two *fanegas*[9] of wheat; an idol of gold, the size of a child four years old [. . .] This treasure was landed on the mole and conveyed to the *Casa de Contratacion*, the vases being carried, and the rest in twenty-six trunks, each cart containing two trunks drawn by a pair of bullocks.[10]

Returning to the ransom, a small part went to Almagro and his 200 comrades who arrived when Pizarro and his men had already carried out the operation. Another part went to Pizarro's eighty comrades left as a garrison at San Miguel; and sailors and merchants who arrived at Cajamarca also received gold. The rest – the greater part of the casting – was divided among the followers of Pizarro, a record of which was carefully compiled and signed. The sixty-four horsemen received on average 8,880 pesos (40.4 kilograms) of good gold and 362 marks of silver (83.4 kilograms); each of the 138 footmen got half those quantities. These amounts would have made them all wealthy men in Spain, though their value in Perú during the early turbulent stages of the Conquest was limited because of the exorbitant prices: a head of garlic cost half a peso of gold, a flagon of wine sixty pesos, a shovel fifty, and a horse 2,500.[11] The lion's share went to Francisco Pizarro who got 57,220 pesos, Hernando Pizarro who got 31,080, and Hernando de Soto (who would later explore the Mississippi) who got 17,740.[12]

The few hundred Spaniards who participated in the first wave of conquest in Perú must have all seen, touched, and acquired gold; and the hope of riches to be wrested out of the rest of that unknown land must have been great. The three Spaniards who went to Cuzco, restricted though they were in their movements by native guides, reported having seen two buildings covered in gold. "There was an object that appeared to be a throne and weighed eight *arrobas* [almost 100 kilograms]; and great fountains that emptied into a small lake that was part of the fountain itself and filled with different kinds of birds and people gathering water, and all this made of gold, a marvelous sight."[13] News of these marvels spread quickly through the Hispanic world on both sides of the Atlantic. The men of Cajamarca were unsure whether to return to Spain and enjoy the wealth they had already accumulated or else stay on in Perú and become wealthier still by the management of prosperous *encomiendas* and the undertaking of further conquests. The value of the loot acquired from the sack of Cuzco, distributed under strict control in March 1534, was about equal to that of Cajamarca.[14] While only a few were able to return soon to Spain – the old, sick, and wounded, and Pizarro's ambassadors – as the bulk of the conquest remained to be completed, about sixty did make their way back over the next couple of years and in all about half ended their days back in Spain.[15]

The stories of gold then were not fables. All had seen it and gotten some. The temples were gilded. The homes of princes and lords were full of gold. The land was vast and populous, and the possibilities for enrichment were real for those willing to face the risks. In 1535, gold was not a myth but a reality, the order of the day and a topic for discussion at court, in homes and taverns, in military encampments, and aboard the ships crossing the ocean.

On another part of the continent and a little while after Cajamarca, 5 April, 1536, to be precise, an expedition of 800 men led by Gonzalo Jiménez de Quesada left from Santa Marta (on the Caribbean coast between Maracaibo Lagoon and the isthmus of Panama) and headed south following the course of the Rio Grande (now known as the Rio Magdalena). The mishaps that attended this expedition were considerably greater than those of Pizarro who had managed to secure the empire with minimal losses. The torrid climate, indigenous attacks, hunger, illness, and accidents combined to reduce Quesada's group to less than a fifth of its original size.[16] Nearly a year after setting out, they arrived on high ground, the plateau inhabited by the Chibchas. This advanced agricultural population included master goldsmiths and was dominated by the two "kingdoms" of Tunja and Bogotá. In particular, the savannah of Bogotá appeared prosperous and rich in salt that was traded for gold with the surrounding populations. Quesada himself visited an emerald mine and saw with his own eyes the extraction of the stones.[17] And while not as abundant as at Cajamarca, there was gold. The *zipa* (king) of Bogotá and the head of the Tunja had both accumulated large treasures, which, however, they managed to keep from the Spaniards. In his report to Oviedo, Quesada wrote: "They use gold for jewelry and to adorn their bodies, on their weapons and for many other things as well, as offerings in their temples, for making idols, and to adorn their dead; and they use their emeralds in similar ways. They take gold from the mines that exist there and emeralds from those places already mentioned and in other places like the lands of the lords of Cacique Somindoco."[18] Cieza de León, who had traversed the length and breadth of that land, wrote: "If there were someone to get it out, one could mine gold and silver there forever, because in the mountains, in the plains, and in the streams, wherever one digs and looks there is gold and silver."[19] The Spaniards obviously lacked the time, inclination, or resources to become prospectors, but there was a quicker way to acquire the precious minerals. The treasure held by the local population must have been large and much of it was stolen or "ransomed" by Quesada's men without any compunction during the months they stayed on the Bogotá savannah. It was a promising region, another Mexico or Perú, and on 6 August, 1538, Quesada founded the city of Santa Fe as first capital of the Kingdom of Nueva Granada (in honor of his homeland), today Bogotá and Colombia respectively.

We must, however, follow the story of Quesada's expedition, similar in various ways to that of other adventurers, to its end in order to understand the origin and rapid spread of the legend of El Dorado. A few weeks after the founding of Bogotá, as Quesada prepared to return to Spain in order to claim lordship over the region, two other expeditions were approaching. The first consisted of 160 men and came over the mountains that separated the Bogotá savannah from the basin of the Orinoco to the east. It was led by Nicolaus Federman who had left from Coro (east of Maracaibo) two years before with a group twice that size. Federman was the agent of the German bankers, the Welsers, who had lent huge sums to Charles V and been awarded exploration rights for the region of Venezuela. The other was led by Sebastián de Benalcázar, one of Pizarro's most trusted and able comrades, who had come up from Quito after having founded Popayán and Cali. He had a similar force, well equipped and with horses and pigs, though it had not undergone the sorts of challenges faced by the other expeditions. The legend of El Dorado spread among Benalcázar's men, reportedly told by an Indio in Quito; it had kindled their imagination as they made their way to the north where the mythical place was meant to be. When the three expeditions met, the legend also spread among Quesada and Federman's men who in turn spread it to other parts of the continent. Quesada, Federman, and Benalcázar meanwhile returned to the court of Spain with large quantities of gold, emeralds, and other precious stones, in addition to their stories. They went there together to establish priority and receive titles and benefits. Enthusiasm for the riches coming from Perú and the other territories and kingdoms of the continent had reached fever pitch, only slightly dimmed by the civil wars that had broken out between the Spanish factions.[20]

Gold fever was rampant as the amount of the precious mineral arriving at the Casa de Contratación in Seville grew steadily. Although production in the Antilles had essentially dried up by then, the average for 1530–40 exceeded 1,000 kilograms per year; for the 1540s it was 2,500 kilograms per year; and in the 1550s it reached a maximum at over 4,000 kilograms per year.[21] But the era of gold was coming to an end as a series of factors made its acquisition progressively more difficult: the plundering of native hoards was more or less complete; the surface and river deposits were essentially used up; and due to the demographic catastrophe suffered by the Indios, the huge quantity of labor used (not very productively) in the early phases of exploration was no longer available. Beginning in the middle of the sixteenth century, gold gave way to silver as the principal source of New World wealth: thanks to the discovery of the rich deposit at the *cerro* of Potosí, the establishment of mines in Mexico, and the discovery of the amalgamation process for refining the metal. In the 1530s, however, the renown of gold was unmatched and so also the myth of El Dorado.

What was the nature of that myth? Its roots lay in the territory of Chibchas (or Muiscas), in the Cundinamarca Cordillera (today in Colombia), that is covered by lagoons the natives considered sacred and into which they threw precious stones and minerals during religious ceremonies. The almost circular Guatavita lagoon, situated at the foot of the mountains and at an altitude of 2,600 meters, was the most famous of these.[22] According to the classic version of the legend, the *cacique* of Guatavita periodically led a retinue to the lagoon. Covered in a special oil, he was coated in gold dust blown onto him through tubes and so presented a resplendent image. A boat awaited him on the shore of the lagoon and into it he embarked together with several priests and a load of jewelry. Four rowers took them to the middle of the lake where the *cacique* dove into the water and came up cleansed of his gilding. The boat and its load of jewels was then sunk. The ritual was repeated on regular occasions. Oviedo, worldly and a bit of a skeptic, recounts the story with a touch of irony:

I asked around why they called this prince or *cacique* or king: Dorado. The Spaniards resident in Santo Domingo who had been in Quito (there were more than ten of them here) say that according to the Indios, this great lord or prince is always covered in gold powder that is as fine as ground salt. And he believes that to wear any other adornment is less beautiful, that to wear ornaments or arms made of gold and worked with a hammer or stamped or made in other ways is vulgar, something that other lords can wear when they want. To cover oneself in gold instead is new, original, unusual, and more costly, since he who coats himself in gold in the morning, washes it off in the evening and so does this every day of the year. Dressed in this fashion he goes about undisturbed and without embarrassment; nor does he make any effort to hide his fine proportions, to which he pays great attention, and so does not wear any other clothing or covering. Personally, I would like to have the "sweeping rights"[23] to the bedroom of this great lord, more than those to the foundry of Perú or any other part of the world. According to the Indios, then, this great lord or king is fabulously wealthy and every morning he covers himself in a fragrant gum or essence and then the gold that has been made into a fine powder for the purpose I have described attaches itself to that unguent so that he is completely covered in gold from the soles of his feet to the top of his head, and so he emerges resplendent like a gold nugget worked by a master artisan. It seems to me that a *cacique* who dresses himself in this way must possess mines rich in this sort of gold.[24]

Yet while the story of El Dorado struck Oviedo as an amusing legend, it had a certain credibility in Nueva Granada. Hernán Pérez de Quesada, the brother of Gonzalo, did some searching along the shores of the lagoon with a degree of success. In 1572 he carried out a partial draining and discovered 12,000 pesos worth of treasure.[25] But where was the true kingdom of El Dorado?

The entire history of the Conquest is filled with fables and myths, both north and south. Columbus was convinced that he had arrived near to Cathay. In 1512 Juan Ponce de León traveled among the Bimini islands (the Keys between Florida and Cuba) spreading stories of "the fountain of youth which made the old young again."[26] Cabeza de Vaca and the survivors of the failed expedition of Pánfilo de Narváez in Florida revived the medieval legend of the "Seven cities of gold of Cíbola" and so inspired the subsequent explorations of Marcos de Niza and Coronado in Sonora and Arizona.

In South America, the search for El Dorado was long an inspiration for exploration and conquest. To put it differently, El Dorado symbolized the search for new wealth: territory with precious stones or metals, populations to enslave, regions on which to stake claim. But it was also a pretext for bankrolling projects, for duping the ignorant, the credulous, or the desperate. The natives almost always encouraged the myth – placing the region of El Dorado beyond high mountain passes or impenetrable jungles or barren plains, beyond a constantly receding line – in hopes of deflecting the imminent risk posed by the bearded Europeans. The foreigners were demanding, violent guests, often hungry and always unpleasant; much better to send them off in search of the myth in distant and elusive lands. One example can stand for a thousand others: the soldiers of Jorge Espira (Hohemut), the German governor for whom Federman was captain, sought in vain to find their way up the Meta river (a tributary of the Orinoco) in order to make their way over the Cordillera, at which point they heard from the Indios there of another nation to the south:

> where pans and urns and all sorts of plates were made of gold and silver [. . .] in the end, the stories they related were such that for the Spaniards [to wait] one hour seemed like a thousand, such was their desire to proceed and their confidence in the great riches that awaited [. . .]. One of the Indios said he had been there and seen with his own eyes the great wealth [. . .] and that it was just a few days walk away.[27]

In the first phase, the myth resided in the vast equatorial region (at least 2 million square kilometers) east of the Cordillera and comprising the basins of the upper Orinoco and the Rio Negro. It was a region defined by the Cordillera to the west, by the Amazon river to the south, and to the east by the meridian (60° west) that passes through Manaus and follows part of the border between Guyana and Venezuela, touching finally the right bank of the Orinoco delta. The great German naturalist Alexander von Humboldt, who began his long scientific exploration of the "equinoctial regions" at the beginning of the nineteenth century, worked his way up the Orinoco to understand, among other things, the mystery of how the basin of that river communicated with that of the Amazon. He too was fascinated with the myth of El Dorado. With Teutonic precision, Humboldt consulted the chronicles of explorations and voyages; native, Spanish,

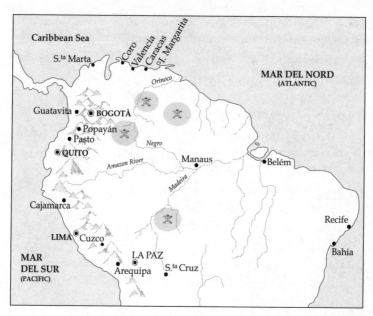

1 The breast-plate symbol indicates the various presumed locations of the mythical El Dorado

and Portuguese place names; and old and new maps, all in order to reconstruct the location of El Dorado according to the beliefs (or fantasies) of the various explorers who had sought it out, from Quesada to Espira to Walter Raleigh.[28] Over the course of the sixteenth century, the location of this imaginary site gradually shifted from the slopes of the eastern Colombian Cordillera to the present-day border between Brazil and British Guyana, 1,500 kilometers to the east. Subsequently, the mythical El Dorado moved further to the south, and expeditions left not only from Colombia and Venezuela, but also Quito, Cuzco, and even Asunción. But before we turn our attention to those southern locales, we should review a bit more the usually disastrous expeditions in the Amazon and Orinoco regions.

We have already described the meeting of the expeditions of

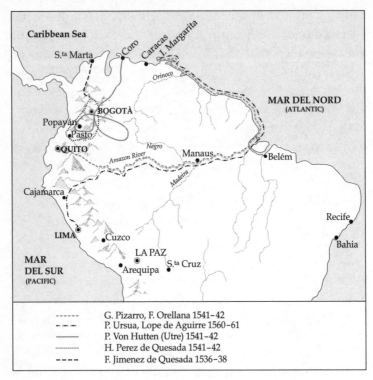

2 Routes taken by various explorers in search of El Dorado

Quesada, Federman, and Benalcázar in the vicinity of Bogotá, the explosion of the myth of El Dorado, and the departure of the trio to Spain, leaving Quesada's brother, Hernán Pérez de Quesada, in command of the region around Bogotá. A stream of colonists and adventurers flowed into the area (including among others Captain Lope de Montalvo and his men who had followed on the heels of Federman); and with them money, arms, horses, and food. Hernán Pérez busied himself preparing an expedition that left in late summer 1541. It consisted of 270 Spaniards, many slaves, 5,000 Indios (twice that number according to another chronicler), 150 horses, and abundant provisions. They crossed over the Cordillera, following the path opened by Federman and Montalvo, made it to the Guaviare (a tributary of the Orinoco), and then plunged into the forest. Hopelessly lost, they headed south, climbed over the mountains and after fifteen months luckily came upon the inhabited valley of Sibundoy, near Pasto (in southern Colombia) and the territory of Benalcázar. The expedition was a failure: no El Dorado, no riches, no lands and peoples to subjugate. Of the 270 Spaniards who started out, 100 were dead; nearly all the slaves and Indios had perished, escaped, or become lost; and only a few horses remained.[29] Hernán Pérez himself met an unusual end. Following the failed expedition, he was arrested by the new governor of Santa Fe and sent as a prisoner to Spain. His ship sailed into a gale on 26 October, 1544, and Hernán Pérez, his younger brother, the captain of the ship, and the bishop of Santa Marta – apparently they were playing cards – were incinerated by a lightning bolt.[30] If it did not take us away from our main concern, it might also be worth recounting the activities of the older Quesada, Francisco Jiménez, when he returned from Spain: the huge failed expedition that he organized as an old man from Bogotá in 1568 (thirty years after its foundation) and the privileges granted to his niece's husband, Antonio de Berrío, so that the latter could continue the undertaking, as in fact he did at the end of the century.[31] Certainly the myth remained a fixation for this family, in spite of repeated failures.

Returning back in time and moving to the north, before Federman met up with Quesada and Benalcázar in Bogotá, various German representatives of the Welsers in Venezuela had attempted to penetrate into the continent from Coro on the coast: first Alfinger (Ehinger) from 1531 to 1533, then Espira (Hohemuth) from 1535 to 1538, and finally Federman who set off in 1536 and arrived in Bogotá three years later, the only one to enjoy success. The expedition of Felipe de Utre (Hutten) followed in this tradition, though it was undertaken after the myth of El Dorado had exploded in Bogotá and while it was still very much in vogue. He departed from Coro in August 1541 with 130 soldiers and an experienced captain in Juan de Limpias; blessed by the bishop, Utre was officially charged with searching for the land of El Dorado.[32] Their route followed that of Espira and Federman; they came upon traces of Hernán Pérez de Quesada's expedition, and, after having crossed the Papamene and reached the upper Caquetá, they learned of the Omagua people. Next they crossed the Guaviare (a tributary of the Orinoco) and were well received by Cacique Macatoa in whose village they rested and obtained provisions, learning also of the fabulous wealth that lay beyond some distant mountains. Vague and fabulous accounts refer to distant sightings of El Dorado but also the impossibility of getting there because of various difficulties and the hostility of the natives, as well as to the wounding of Utre and the exploits of Juan de Limpias who, with thirty-eight men, managed to defeat 15,000 Omaguas, an event that became famous in popular legend. The ending, though, was tragic: Juan de Limpias betrayed Utre who in turn returned to Coro where he was tried and executed by the usurping new governor; the latter himself was subsequently hanged.[33] For our purposes, the primary interest of this account lies not so much in the story of the expedition itself, a narrative in which reality and fantasy intermingle, but in the fact that the expedition was officially commissioned to discover El Dorado; and still more in the fact that there would continue to be reports of wealthy populations adorned all in gold somewhere in the vast region between the western slope of the Cordillera and the Orinoco. Humboldt himself believed that the Guaypes, who lived around the Uaupés river, were the people encountered by Utre and that the gold could have come from deposits on the western Cordillera that had been carried down to the valley by the streams.[34]

El Dorado then was hard to reach. Getting there required crossing the Cordillera at an altitude of 4–5,000 meters; climbing down the valleys of the Orinoco tributaries on the other side; navigating swollen rivers and floods; crossing the tropical forests; defending oneself against suspicious and hostile Indios; avoiding poisonous arrows, caimans, and insects; and surviving hunger, injuries, and illness. Such was the attraction, though, that even a figure of Gonzalo Pizarro's stature, youngest brother of Francisco and named by him governor of Quito, was sent beyond the Cordillera to "search for cinnamon and a great prince whom they call Dorado." Cinnamon (or *Cinnamomum zeylanicum*), a tree whose bark was much sought after, had been found in the region around Quito. Gonzalo arrived there in 1540 and took several months (and 50,000 pesos in gold) to organize his expedition which consisted of a crew of 210 men, the usual massive following of 4,000 Indios, as well as 4–5,000 pigs, 1,000 dogs, and herds of llama for food and transport. Some time after their departure, a rearguard followed.[35] The expedition departed in February 1541 and, losing many Indios who died from cold and hardship, crossed over the Cordillera and descended into the valley of the Coca river (part of the Amazon system); from there they plunged into the forest which quickly proved intractable for an expedition of that size. The Indios fled or died, as did the horses; animals and provisions alike were lost. A great deal of time was taken up in explorations, in sending out missions to find the right path, and in continually wandering about. They found very few cinnamon trees. Around November they reached the banks of the Coca, and Pizarro instructed one of his captains, Francisco de Orellana, to construct a brigantine – employing the craftsmen who accompanied the expedition – and sail down the river in search of supplies. The Coca flows into the Napo, one of the major tributaries of the

Amazon. Orellana embarked with fifty-seven men, including the Dominican Gaspar de Carvajal who would be the chronicler of the expedition, and instructions to turn back after twelve days. After a long and fruitless wait and further explorations, Pizarro turned wearily back toward Quito, where he would arrive in August 1542, having lost half of his men and most of his horses; not a single Indio returned with him. The expedition was a total loss. Having penetrated only a short way into the unknown lands east of the Andes, they found neither riches, nor cinnamon, nor populations to subjugate, nor lands suitable for colonization.[36]

The story of Orellana is well known, both because it is so extraordinary and because of the chronicle penned by Carvajal after his return, an account that falls somewhere between truth and fable.[37] After leaving Pizarro, Orellana and his men navigated down the Coca and the Napo rivers to where the latter joined the Amazon; they then sailed the entire length of the Amazon, struck out into the "Mar del Nord," and finally dropped anchor at the island of Cubagua on 11 September, 1542, after a trip of over 6,000 kilometers. Carvajal's chronicle, among other things, offered support to Orellana who claimed not to have obeyed the order to turn back after twelve days because of unforeseen obstacles.

Carvajal's report includes both precise and verifiable information – for example, a list of the men who took part in the voyage – and wild inventions, likely to be believed only by credulous and unsophisticated readers. It includes, for example, the blending of the myth of gold and the older one of the Amazons. Columbus himself had reported (in January 1493 after he returned from his first voyage) that the natives of Santo Domingo described a strange island of Matininó "inhabited only by women and where there was much gold."[38] Carvajal's description of the Amazons begins with an account of a battle with river-dwelling Indios during a stop on the Amazon river to forage for food, probably by sacking a few villages:

> More than an hour was taken up in this fight, for the Indians did not lose spirit, rather it seemed as if it was being doubled in them, although they saw many of their own numbers killed, and they passed over them [i.e. their bodies], and they merely kept retreating and coming back again. I want it to be known what the reason was why these Indians defended themselves in this manner. It must be explained that they are the subjects of, and tributaries to, the Amazons, and, our coming having been made known to them, they went to them to ask help, and there came as many as ten or twelve of them, for we ourselves saw these women, who were there fighting in front of all the Indian men as women captains, and these latter fought so courageously that the Indian men did not dare to turn their backs, and anyone who did turn his back they killed with clubs right there before us, and this is the reason why the Indians kept up their defense for so long. These women are very white and tall, and have hair very long and braided and wound around the head, and they are very robust and go about naked, [but] with their privy parts covered, with their bows and arrows in their hands, doing as much fighting as ten Indian men, and indeed there was one woman among those who shot an arrow a span deep into one of the brigantines, and others less deep, so that our brigantines looked like porcupines.[39]

A truly extraordinary event. A few days later Orellana, who knew a bit of the language, tried to learn more from an Indio whom they had taken prisoner:

> the Captain took [aside] the Indian who had been captured further back [. . .] and asked him of what place he was native:

the Indian answered that he was from that village where
he been seized; the Captain asked him what the name of
the overlord of this land was, and the Indian replied that
his name was Couynco and that he was a very great overlord and that his rule extended to where we were, and that,
as I have already said, was [a stretch of] one hundred and
fifty leagues. The Captain asked him what women those
were [who] had come to help them and fight against us; the
Indian said that they were certain women who resided in the
interior of the country, a seven day journey from the shore,
and [that] it was because this overlord Couynco was subject
to them that they had come to watch over the shore. The
Captain asked him if these women were married: the Indian
said that they were not. The Captain asked him about how
they lived: the Indian replied [first] that, as he had already
said, they were off in the interior of the land and that he
had been there many times and had seen their customs and
mode of living, for as their vassal he was in the habit of
going there to carry the tribute whenever the overlord sent
him. The Captain asked if these women were numerous: the
Indian said they were, and that he knew by name seventy
villages, and named them before those of us who were there
present, and [he added] that he had been in several of them.
The Captain asked him if [the houses in] these villages were
built of straw: the Indian said that they were not, but out of
stone and with regular doors, and that from one village to
another went roads closed off on one side and on the other
and with guards stationed at intervals along them so that no
one might enter without paying duties. The Captain asked
if these women bore children: the Indian answered that
they did. The Captain asked him how, not being married
and there being no man residing among them, they became
pregnant: he said that these Indian women consorted with
Indian men at times, and, when that desire came to them,

they assembled a great horde of warriors and went off to make war on a very great overlord whose residence is not far from that [i.e. the land] of these women, and by force they brought them to their own country and kept them with them for the time that suited their caprice, and after they found themselves pregnant, they sent them back to their country without doing them any harm; and afterwards, when the time came for them to have children, if they gave birth to male children, they killed them or sent them to their fathers, and, if female children, they raised them with great solemnity and instructed them in the arts of war. He said furthermore that among all these women there was one ruling mistress who subjected and held under her hand and jurisdiction all the rest, which mistress went by the name of Coñori. He said that there was [in their possession] a very great wealth of gold and silver and that [in the case of] all the mistresses of rank and distinction their eating utensils were nothing but gold or silver, while the other women, belonging to the plebeian class, used a service of wooden vessels, except what was brought in contact with fire, which was of clay. He said that in the capital and principal city in which the ruling mistress resided there were houses dedicated to the Sun, which they called "caranain," and [that] inside, from half a man's height above the ground up, these buildings were lined with heavy wooden ceilings covered with paint of various colors, and that in these buildings they had many gold and silver idols in the form of women, and many vessels of gold and of silver for the service of the Sun; and these women were dressed in clothing of very fine wool, because in this land there are many sheep of the same sort as those of Peru; their dress consisted of blankets girded about them [covering their bodies] from the breasts down, [in some cases merely] thrown over [the shoulders], and in others clasped together in front, like a cloak, by means of a pair of cords; they wore their hair reaching down to the ground at their feet, and upon their heads [were] placed crowns of gold, as wide as two fingers [. . .] He related that they had a rule to the effect that when the sun went down no male Indian was to remain [anywhere] in all the cities, but that any such must depart and go to his country; he said in addition that many Indian provinces bordering on them were held in subjection by them and made to pay tribute and to serve them, while other [provinces] there were with which they carried on war, in particular with the one we have mentioned, and they brought the men [of this province] there to have relations with them: these were said to be of very great stature and white and numerous.[40]

In the fantastic story written by Carvajal, the myth of gold coexists with that of the Amazons and that of wealthy and civilized populations (perhaps the Inca) who had migrated from the west across the Cordillera. And while Oviedo may have ridiculed the story – he noted that Orellana's Amazons did not need to burn off one breast in order to use their bows like mythical Amazons – it is possible that others believed in this amazing land or at least the part that had to do with gold. Certainly Orellana wanted to try again, and after returning home, he obtained the governorship of Marañón and armed an expedition of 400 men to go "in search of those Amazons whom he had never seen but made much of when back in Spain."[41] He did arrive again at the mouth of the Amazon river and then died there along with most of his company.

Legends about the lands beyond the Andes spread quickly to the south, and a number of expeditions were organized in hopes of discovering new opportunities for wealth and power. While the German captains representing the Welsers started out from Coro and Quesada left from Santa Marta (on the Caribbean coasts of Venezuela and Colombia respectively),

Hernán Pérez de Quesada set off from Bogotá, and Gonzalo Pizarro and Francisco de Orellana from Quito in Ecuador. Other expeditions crossed the Andes farther to the south. El Dorado lay not only on the left bank of the Amazon basin, but was imagined most anywhere beyond the mountains.

There were of course other factors as well that encouraged more than one enterprising adventurer to organize further expeditions. In 1538 the struggle between the Pizarros and Diego de Almagro, who had been Francisco Pizarro's powerful associate from the beginning of the Peruvian enterprise, reached a conclusion. The Pizarro faction emerged victorious after the Battle of Salinas (1538, near Quito), and Almagro was beheaded. Yet the civil war that would rage in Perú for many years had only just begun. Cuzco seethed with captains and soldiers from the two factions; not only the victors and the vanquished but also unsatisfied victors, elements from the losing side waiting to avenge their loss, and of course members of both groups in search of wealth. While Francisco was in Lima, Hernando Pizarro thought it a good idea to ease up the pressure on the city – only recently freed from a long revolt and siege by the Indios – by issuing licenses for exploration and conquest to a number of ambitious captains. Pedro de Candía (about whom we shall have more to say) was among these:

> and many of the one and the other went with him, that is of the Pizarro band and the Almagro band [. . .] and others went with Alonso de Alvarado to the lands of the Chachapoyas, and others with Alonso de Mercadillo to the Guancachupados, and others with Captain Vergara to the Bracamoros, and others still with Orellana to the Culata [Bay] of San Miguel where the Puna Island lies.[42]

It is unclear how effective Hernando Pizarro's policy ultimately was, but there is no doubt that almost all of the expeditions ended up suffering huge losses of life (Spaniards, of course, but above all Indios).

The expedition organized by Alonso de Alvarado got underway in 1538 in northern Perú, near Cajamarca.[43] Alvarado founded the city of Chachapoyas, 30 leagues to the north-east of Cajamarca. Having crossed over the western Cordillera and arrived at the Huallaga river, a tributary to the Marañón (the upper Amazon): "He had news that fifteen days' journey beyond the river after passing a great and rough forest, one came to a level country, where there was a great lake, upon the banks of which lived a noble of Inca lineage named Ancallas, besides others who were very great and rich."[44] Alvarado turned back when he got news of an Indian rebellion in Chachapoyas, leaving the search for this El Dorado to his brother who forded the river, plunged into the forest, and reached the mountains, but then had to turn back, suffering the usual adversities and casualties.

Pedro de Candía was one of the earliest and closest of Pizarro's companions; he was one of the thirteen men who suffered seven months of hunger with Pizarro on Gallo Island in 1527. A large man of Greek origin, clever and inclined to boast, he was an expert with firearms and artillery and on arrival at Tumbez hit a target with an harquebus to the amazement of the natives there. He played a major role in the ransom of Atahuallpa and further enriched himself at Cuzco where he was appointed *alcalde* from the city's foundation (1534). Of great renown, he possessed a valuable *encomienda*.[45] It was said that

according to information he had from an Indio woman, there lay a rich and populous land beyond the Andes called Ambata. Rashly he asked for a license to seek out that land, and Hernando Pizarro happily granted it, perceiving the

3 Map by Vander (mid-sixteenth century)

opportunity to distance some of those proud and terrible men who posed a constant threat to public order.

Outfitting the mission was extravagantly expensive: Pedro spent 85,000 pesos of his own and borrowed a similar sum in order to field 300 well-equipped soldiers. The latter figured that if Pedro de Candía was spending so much money, he must know where he was going and so they would get rich; and even if the expedition was a failure, they had nothing to lose so they left in good spirits.

Among the 300, Hernando Pizarro had placed many followers of Almagro. They left in early 1538 and began "a march to reach the other side of the Cordillera, commonly referred to as the Andes, traveling to the east and toward the Mar del Nord to an area bounded on the north by the Opotari river and on the south by the Cochabamba Valley which they call the entrance to the Mojos" (much of the rest of this book will deal with the Mojos). They continued "with great difficulty, coming upon many lofty mountains and thick forests where one never sees the sun or even a clearing as there are always rain and storms." Finally,

they arrived at the most difficult and dangerous place they had yet encountered, because there was a steep mountain covered with thick brush. Thick vines hung from the trees which slowed and even blocked the passage of the horses, and finding themselves in a desperate situation, they did not know what to do. God, who always helps his own, awoke the ingenuity of these men so that they could come up with a solution. They cut the long vines and made ropes out of them, and the younger and more agile among them clambered up the slope, tied the ropes to trees, and with incredible difficulty used them to haul up the horses.[46]

· They crossed over the Cordillera and descended into a torrid zone on the other side, where the forest was so thick that they had to clear their passage with hatchets and machetes. They crossed streams and swamps on thrown-together bridges and rafts and survived Indian attacks; yet still they marched on:

> every day a little more or less than a league, constantly tor-
> mented by the many thorns they encountered. For although
> they proceeded with great caution, they were assailed by
> the sharp points that pricked their feet and legs so that they
> swelled up, as the thorns were poisonous. Crossing streams
> and swamps and rocky areas, their suffering was great as
> many were slashed with wounds and it was hard to see them
> suffering for many different reasons, and they were hungry
> too and ate the horses that died. The rivers they came upon
> were deep and they had to fell trees and make bridges with
> vines and use branches to fill the swamps and puddles and
> though wearisome they were great masters at this.[47]

A few months after setting out, they succeeded in retracing their steps and crossing back over the Cordillera to the plateau. There were only a few Spanish casualties, while all the Indios either disappeared or perished. The investment meanwhile was a total loss, and all dreams of wealth disappointed. We know nothing about the captivating Indian woman who gave such poor advice. We do know, however, that Pedro left a *mestizo* son who would be a friend of Garcilaso de la Vega. Back in Cuzco four years later, when the son of Almagro was waging war against the Pizarros, Candía – who by then had abandoned the Pizarro faction – was employed together with his gang of Greeks to build cannons and harquebuses. He carried out his commission, but in the Battle of Chupas was accused by Almagro himself of betrayal and executed.

One of Candía's captains was Pedro Anzures or Peranzures. When the expedition re-emerged on the plateau, Pizarro received warning that the Almagro faction was plotting against him and set out to meet the beleaguered company. On arrival, he executed the suspected head of the faction, sent Candía to Cuzco, and assigned the survivors to Peranzures with orders to undertake another expedition, this time into the land of the Chunchos, "barbarian" Indios who lived beyond the Cordillera east of Cuzco in a low and forested region. Following the advice of informants, Peranzures thought to find "thickly-peopled country rich in gold and silver, so that they might all return in prosperity to Spain."[48] Peranzures and his men "crossed over the Cordillera passing through Carabaya and exploring the path that leads from Apolombamba and San Juan del Oro to the east. In this way they arrived in the land of the Chunchos who live in the basin of the Beni River."[49] The expedition left in September 1538 and returned several months later. According to one chronicler, 153 of the 300 or so Spaniards of the original company had died, along with about 4,000 Indios; 220 horses had died and been eaten.[50] Before a magistrate, Rodrigo de Quiroga, a respected member of the expedition, testified that:

> The soldiers were dying three or four at a time, exhausted, worn, and ill from fatigue and hunger; they died in one another's arms [. . .] Of the 300 Spaniards who set out, not more than 80 returned [. . .] and when they arrived at Larecaxa they kissed the ground. They were naked with their lacerated feet and shoulders and so emaciated and disfigured as to be unrecognizable.[51]

The indefatigable Peranzures enjoyed more success than Pedro de Candía, as rather than return to Cuzco he acquired reinforcements and headed south with his expedition. He passed a spot near the Illimani peak (which would later become La Paz), but it did not appeal to him, so he continued on and founded the city of Chuquisaca or La Plata (today Sucre, the administrative capital of Bolivia). He then turned back and founded Arequipa at the feet of the Misti volcano.[52]

The Cuzco expeditions did not go much beyond the land of the Mojos, focus of the chapters that follow; it lies in the upper basin of the Madeira river, one of the major tributaries on the right bank of the Amazon. The several expeditions described in these pages were neither the only nor the last ones and others were undertaken in the decades that followed, including famous and dramatic examples like that of Pedro de Ursúa or of the rebellious and mad Lope de Aguirre along the Amazon river.

There are a number of reasons, though, for halting our review at this point: the other adventures, though varied, are fairly repetitive in their outlines; geographically we have arrived at the area of primary interest to us; and in subsequent expeditions the mania for El Dorado began to subside and get mixed up with the more mundane goals of exploration, conquest, and settlement. Moreover, in the late 1530s and early 1540s other political factors also came to play a role, namely the strategy of sending off members of hostile factions on distant explorations. Later on, in the latter part of the century, the Crown and its viceroys also sought to contain infiltration of Portuguese coming from Brazil. And in 1550, at the end of the civil wars, a royal *Cédula* (decree) forbade the concession of licenses for exploration, perhaps to avoid further depletion of the country's resources after a quarter-century of conflict: Indios against Indios, Spaniards against Indios, and Spaniards against Spaniards. That decree was neither absolute nor definitive, but it marked the end of an era.[53]

In any case, the heroic phase of exploration was nearly over by 1550. Cieza de León, who was surely the greatest and most careful chronicler of the Conquest of South America and, departing from the Caribbean coast, had traveled the length and breadth of Perú, was skeptical about the eastern explorations. A soldier, voyager, and chronicler with direct experience of places, facts, and people, he wrote around 1550:

> The Cordillera or ridge of the mountains we call the Andes begins at the Straits of Magellan and crosses many lands and provinces, as I have written in my description of these lands. And we know that on the side facing the Mar del Sur (the western side), there is great wealth in most of the rivers and valleys, while the lands and provinces on the eastern side are lacking in metals according to the conquistadors who have come from the Rio de la Plata [. . .] Those who explored the region with the Captains Diego de Rojas, Felipe Gutierrez, and Nicolas de Heredia found no wealth at all. After entering into the lands beyond the Cordillera of the Andes, where Gonzalo Pizarro had sent him, the Adelantado Francisco de Orellana sailed down the Marañón River in search of cinnamon; and though the Spaniards frequently came upon large villages they saw little or no gold and silver. And there is really little more to be said on the topic, because aside from the province of Bogotá in no other part of the Andes Cordillera [the eastern side] has any wealth at all been found. The situation in the south is entirely different, as the greatest riches and treasures the world has seen in many epochs have been found there. And if the gold that was in the provinces bordering on the Rio Grande de Santa Marta, from Popayán to the city of Mopox, were all in the hands of a single lord, as was the case in the province of Perú, his greatness would exceed that of Cuzco.[54]

From Cieza's point of view, it was pointless to look for El Dorado east of the Andes.

The expeditions were costly. They required money, men, porters, horses and pack animals, herds of animals for food, arms, and equipment of all sorts. Especially in the early years, men were scarce and costs high. The captains of the expeditions required a *"capitulación"* granted by the king, a viceroy, or governor. The *capitulación* gave the captain the office of *adelantado* or governor of the territories to discover and settle, along with other privileges for himself and his sons. But the captain (and his partners if he had any) had to advance all the expenses of the expedition (that is why they were called *adelantados*, from *adelantar*, to advance): tens of thousands of pesos in gold, sums that only the wealthiest commanded. Captains, subalterns, and soldiers received no pay at all; at most they received their arms, horses, and food. Organization of the expedition depended then upon the anticipated booty to be gotten through conquest: gold, silver, and precious stones if they were found (and after having subtracted the *"quinto"* owed to the Crown); territories and populations to subjugate with the goods, taxes, and services that might accrue. Failure could mean financial ruin; the rare success, power and wealth.[55]

From the stories of the chroniclers, often exaggerated and embellished but all with an element of truth, we can deduce that the human costs of the expeditions were enormous. Each of them was accompanied by a contingent of Indios whose size was about ten times that of the Spanish company. Domingo de Santo Tomás wrote: "Two or three hundred Spaniards took part in these expeditions. They took with them two or three thousand Indios as servants and porters of food and provisions, and everything was carried on the shoulders of these poor Indios [. . .]. Few or none of the Indios survived, because of the shortage of food, the great hardship of long voyages across desolate regions, and the weight of their loads."[56] Santo Tomás's account coincides fairly well with other reports and chronicles; though to these hardships we should add, a fact unknown to the first wave of Spaniards, the vulnerability of the Indios to dramatic changes in altitude and temperature. The Incas by comparison had been well aware of this factor and organized the many migrations planned out in their colonization programs to transfer population between areas with similar geo-climates and avoid altitude changes. For the populations of the plateau, scaling the Cordillera at over 5,000 meters to then descend into the torrid lowlands to the east carried high risks. Though smaller in scale, the Spanish losses were also significant; their expeditions often returned depleted by half or two-thirds. Yet they surely understood the risk they were running and must have been willing to do so in the expectation of great wealth. In this fatal game of high risks and wagers, charity toward the native populations was the clear loser. The activities of the Spaniards – initially just a few hundred – were successful insofar as they were able to subjugate a multitude of Indios for service, transport, exploration, the building of cities, and military campaigns. That subjugation was among the important causes behind the demographic catastrophe of the Indios.

II

AT THE FOOT OF THE ANDES, UNDER WATER
FOR FIVE MONTHS OF THE YEAR. THE
INHABITANTS OF THE GREAT SWAMP: MILD,
INGENIOUS, ADAPTABLE. THREE MEN IN A
BOAT TAKE A CENSUS. VAST QUANTITIES OF
LAND AND WATER, BUT NO GOLD, SILVER,
OR PRECIOUS STONES

The distance between Santa Marta on the Caribbean coast of Colombia, whence departed Quesada's expedition, and Cuzco, the starting point for Pedro de Candía and Peranzures a few years later, is 2,800 kilometers as the crow flies; and probably over 4,000 following the shortest path between the two. In 1541, Pedro de Valdivia founded Santiago in Chile, 2,200 kilometers south of Cuzco. In a mere six years, then, the entire western slope of the Andes, from north of the equator to the temperate regions in the south (from 11° N latitude to 34° S), had been traversed, explored, and settled. The search for El Dorado – or more realistically, the search for new lands and peoples and possibly wealth – had led to the exploration of the Orinoco river, the scaling of the Andes by numerous costly and almost always disastrous expeditions, and the navigation of the Amazon river for 6,000 kilometers to its estuary in the Atlantic ocean. Little or nothing of value had been found, but the adventure continued, pushing southward, inspired by the same motivations and colored by new myths. Those myths, as we shall see, acquired new names: not just El Dorado, but also the Grand Mojo and Paititi. In chapter III we shall trace the growing awareness that these were indeed nothing but myths; as a result the explorations and expeditions altered in scope, seeking souls to convert to the true faith rather than Indios to kidnap and enslave. The adventuresome Spaniards gradually discovered that further to the south, beyond the Andes, there were neither mines rich in gold nuggets, nor *caciques* covered in gold, nor temples – as there had been in Cuzco – covered in tiles of precious metal.

The region of Llanos de Mojos – Llanos or 'plains' and Mojos or Moxos from the name of one of the ethnic groups that lived there – is located in the upper basin of the Madeira river (a major tributary of the Amazon); it is flooded for much of the year, has a damp hot climate not well suited to human settlement, and lacks natural resources. Long unknown, it nonetheless inspired fantasies and legends. It is to this region that we now turn. Its inhabitants consisted of a few tens of thousands of Indios spread among small settlements, who cultivated cassava, hunted, and above all fished. Their manufactured goods were few, their social organization simple, and their linguistic variety remarkable. They engaged in the occasional inter-ethnic skirmish.[1] Given this uninviting terrain, the interest of both Spaniards and Portuguese for the region is surprising, as is the fact that the Jesuits created there a network of missions that was second only to the thirty missions of Paraguay, both in terms of demographic importance and organization. Equally of note, while the missions fell into disrepair after the Company of Jesus was expelled in 1767, gradually swallowed up by the jungle, and the faithful were dispersed, the population of the Llanos survived in spite of numerous crises:

> The Mojos were in fact decimated 200 years after their subjugation, due to the free market in rubber, but they did not disappear and continue to live, entirely integrated, in that region which enjoys the richest agriculture of Bolivia. Their churches, unlike those of the Guaraní, have not been reduced to the ruins of a glorious past, but instead many still stand and protect within them the descendants of those who built them three centuries ago.[2]

But rather than get ahead of ourselves, we should attempt to understand, based on documents and descriptions, the natural and human context the Europeans sought to penetrate. The Llanos de Mojos correspond approximately to the present-day department of Beni in northern Bolivia.[3] Its natural borders include the slopes of the Andes to the south-west, the Chiquitos Heights to the south-east, to the north-east the Brazilian plateau on the right bank of the Rio Iténez (or Guaporé) which marks the border between Bolivia and Brazil, and the Rio Madre de Dios to the north-west (see map 4). This flat region forms a basin traversed by numerous rivers, the largest of which (the Madre de Dios, the Beni, the Mamoré, the Iténez or Guaporé) form a dense network well adapted to riverine communication. To the north, the rivers of the basin flow into the Madeira, one of the principal tributaries on the right bank of the Amazon, which makes its way there by cutting a series of non-navigable rapids through the Brazilian terrain. Santa Cruz de la Sierra lies to the south, 100 miles from the plain and at an elevation of 600 meters,

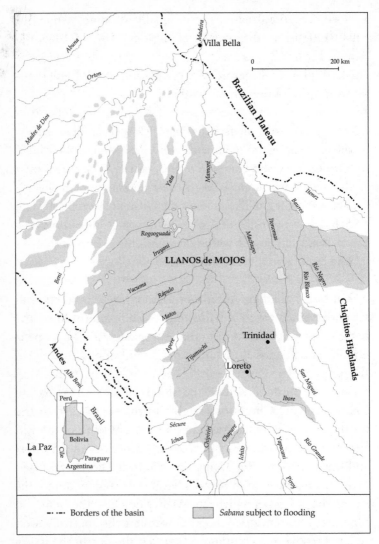

4 *The Llanos de Mojos and the areas subject to flooding*

and constitutes a point of access to the region by way of the Guapay river (or Rio Grande, which flows northward into the Mamoré). As one can see from the map, the Andes pose a formidable obstacle to anyone attempting to reach the region from Alto Perú (present-day western Bolivia). The Spaniards preferred a route that followed the Guapay, which originates near Cochabamba and flows to the south carving a broad arc through the Cordillera before turning north-ward and flowing into the Madeira. Santa Cruz de la Sierra was founded along this route. The Llanos are studded with floodplains and shallow permanent swamps. Excluding the Andean slopes and Chiquitos Heights, the entire region lies between 200 and 300 meters of altitude. It covers 180,000 square kilometers, four fifths of which lie under water for several months of each year. Present-day organization of the territory – with roads, levees, drainage, and canals – has drastically reduced the flooding. The rainy season begins in October–November and ends in April. The dry season lasts from May to September. Heavy rains (between 1,500 and 2,000 mm per year, with maxima of 2,800 mm at the foot of the Andes) lead to overflowing rivers and floods that peak in February and begin to recede in March. According to the lay of the land, the stagnant water lasts from a few weeks to six months:[4] "All business except that conducted by canoe comes to a halt."[5]

In flooded areas, the depth of the water could range from a few centimeters to a couple of meters; historically, disastrous floods seem to have come about five times each century. In the summer (October–April), the climate is rainy, humid, and hot; in the winter (May–September) it is dry, often with southerly winds that can push the temperature down below 10°C, uncomfortably cold for the Indios. Alcides D'Orbigny, who traveled the length and breadth of the region in the 1820s, said that when the days were clear – during his navigation among the wild rivers – the heat was unbearable and one awaited the relief that night would bring, "but when night arrived, a dense fog rose from the rivers, and by morning one was soaked through as though it had poured down rain all the night," and when it actually rained "thousands of mosquitoes came out of the woods and found refuge on the canoes where they tortured the unfortunate travelers."[6]

About half of the Llanos consists of pampas that flood for long periods; the vegetation is mostly grasses and the terrain of limited fertility and not much use for agriculture. Scattered among the pampas are small natural wooded elevations. The highest parts of the Llanos, in particular the eastern and western edges of the basin, are forested and do not flood. In between is savannah with grass, bushes, and the occasional tree. One finds traces of native efforts to reshape the terrain: raised areas for travel during the floods, cultivation, and settlement, and canals for boat travel. The landscape has undergone rapid changes with the passage of time. During the rainy season, the course of the rivers may change as much sediment is washed down from the Andes, shifting the rivers, forming new lakes and floodplains, or changing their shape. The geography of settlement then has to change as well and has varied considerably over the centuries. The earliest missionaries were made aware of the changeable nature of the rivers during a first long stay at a Mojo village situated on the banks of a river "which wiped out the village where the Fathers were staying when it overflowed its high banks and carved out a new bed through which to flow."[7] Father Orellana, moreover, "had heard of an old Indio who in more than sixty years could only remember once that five years passed during which the river did not change course."[8] And Altamirano noted: "There is an Indio who in less than six years has lived in four different villages and is now changing once more."[9] The thick network of streams facilitated travel and transport, for the most part via canoe. Around 8 to 10 leagues (42–55 kilometers) could be covered in a day going upstream, and twice that coming back down with the current,[10] though much depended on the skill of the oarsmen and the speed of the current. The Loreto and Trinidad missions were 36 leagues apart, a two-day trip by river.[11] Father Julian de Aller took eleven days to reach his brother friars, traveling down the Guapay and covering 120 leagues (660 kilometers).[12] In 1767, at the time of the expulsion of the Jesuits, a flotilla of forty-three canoes including a military detachment brought the new priests and carried away the dismissed Jesuits; it took a month and a half to travel 1,000 kilometers (round trip) during the unfavorable dry season and making many stops along the way.[13]

The original settlements were fragmented and dispersed throughout the territory, before the Jesuits imposed their "reductions" into larger concentrations of population. Generally speaking the villages were situated near streams – the principal avenues of transportation – on raised land (*islas*) that was not systematically flooded and on which it was possible to practice a rudimentary slash-and-burn agriculture and the growing of cassava and maize. Nonetheless, flooding and the shifting rivers made life hard for these people. Turning again to Father Orellana:

> [Flooding] was the cause of all suffering because the stream, leaving its banks, flooded everything. Water covered the fields and caused the yucca to rot which meant calamity for them, because if they do not have the bread and the beverage they make from it, they suffer terribly. And that suffering will last for a year as until the water recedes, they cannot sew their seeds and after the sewing it takes a year before the plant bears fruit. And should another flood follow on the first one? Then the suffering will last yet another year.

The flooding, moreover, disrupted the equilibria of their day-to-day lives, as the water:

> entered their houses and forced them to live on top of the *barbacoas* [platforms] day and night and without protection from the mosquitoes, as the round huts they had built to defend themselves from those annoying insects had become uninhabitable, and never were the swarms denser than during the floods. And so they were helpless victims day and night, stranded on the *barbacoas* from which they only left by canoe; for while the water was shallow, they nonetheless feared being bitten by piranhas. They lacked wood as well that they could only gather by climbing up the trees in search of dry branches that they broke off with the strength of their arms, as they did not have appropriate tools. And so while there was an abundance of fish and game, much of it rotted as they could not roast it – their method of preservation given that they had no salt – because of the lack of wood. These calamities afflicted not just the men but also the animals as they could find nowhere to sleep and drowned in the woods and the fields. And so the natives suffered still more as when the waters receded the fields were filled with the dead deer, boar, and other game on which they normally depended, and so the hunger was still greater. And pestilence followed, inevitable companion, born of the corruption of the air by so much putrefaction.[14]

This vivid description helps us to understand the obstacles that nature imposed not so much on survival in the Llanos – as there was plenty of food – but on the stable and structured lives of the inhabitants. "Thus change and disaster are common in Mojos, and man has learned to live with them, to adapting and to recover."[15]

Travelers, both today and in the past, testify to the

enormous natural changes that take place during the annual weather cycle, changes that have a profound impact on the lives of the people there. With the coming of the rainy summer, the countryside is everywhere verdant. Then, as the rivers overflow, the swamps and floodplains expand into lakes dotted with *islas* and curved strips of wooded land. The floodplains teem with fish, and the sky is filled with flocks of different sorts of birds, as men and animals congregate on the dry areas and live an amphibious life. A dramatic change then comes with the dry season.

> The marshes first become muddy and are filled with stagnant pools, rotting dead fish, and rank grasses; and then they dry out completely. Rains are infrequent, many trees lose their leaves, the grasses turns brown, and the clay soils crack. The aerial view is one of tall pampa grasses, scattered scrub trees and palms, and forest patches. The *bajios* and small rivers dry up, but the shallow rectangular lakes persist. The trails become dusty, and grass fires fill the sky with smoke. The aspect is one of bleak grayness and aridity. Overland movement is easy, but water is at a premium; birds migrate north and mammals move toward the permanent lakes and rivers. For the traveler who has seen the Llanos during flooding it is disconcerting to return in August and find water brought many miles by oxcart to be sold in towns and to see canoes tied up to the hitching post of a ranch house with the nearest body of water many miles away.[16]

The people whom the Spaniards encountered in the Llanos were divided into a variety of ethnicities. Many of these descended from the Arawaks, including the Mojos, who gave their name to the region, and the Baures. They had come from the north, making their way up the rivers.

According to William Denevan, this plurality of ethnicities in the upper river basins argues in favor of the theory that the direction of migration was from the valley toward the mountains. In the valleys, where there is less diversity, the stronger groups forced the weaker ones to relocate and so move upstream. The majority groups, the Mojos and the Baures, spoke an Arawak language and were presumably "recent" arrivals, while the other groups – Movimas, Itonomas, Cayuvavas, and Canichanas - are thought to have been there earlier and spoke a variety of languages (see map 5). The Mojos, Baures, and Cayuvavas were more structured populations, organized in villages, and possessing a degree of social stratification. The Movimas and Itonomas were more simply organized, while the Canichanas were nomadic warriors with little in the way of agriculture.[17] The list of tribes and ethnicities recorded by the first Jesuits to visit the region is considerably longer and more complex than this sketch and includes dozens of names.[18] As we shall see, the work of conversion and reduction of the population into villages led to the disappearance of most of the smaller groups, either by mixing, extinction, or flight into the forest.

The inhabitants of the Llanos enjoyed ample sources of food. On the raised areas that did not flood, they practiced slash-and-burn agriculture and grew yucca (their primary food), maize, potatoes, beans, and cotton.[19] "Because of the flooding and the scarcity of land free of this calamity, agriculture is practiced in the woods and on the raised land next to the streams. Given the make-up of the land, there are fields that lie two or three days distant from the house or village."[20] Hunting, and especially fishing, were rich sources of animal protein, especially after the flooding stopped.

Swarms of prized fish swim in the lagoons and rivers, offering themselves up to hook or net. There are many sorts of

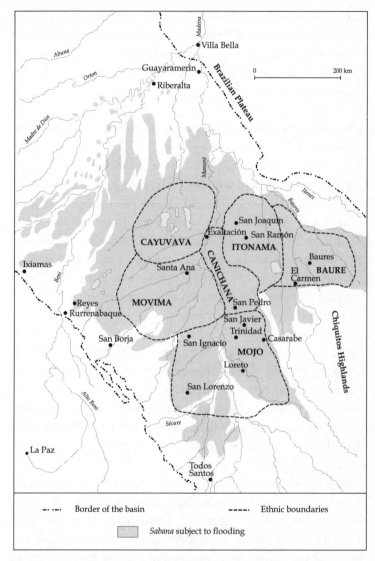

5 Settlements of the principal ethnicities of the Llanos de Mojos

duck, dove, turkey, pheasant and other birds that are pleas-
ing to see and hear as well as to eat. The woods are filled
with *anta*, boar, deer, and hare, as well as those animals that
are not eaten, but who are themselves predators, like snakes
and jackals.[21]

According to Diego Francisco Altamirano, the Mojos diet
included:

> several varieties of beans, boar, deer, hare, rabbit, monkey,
> *quirquincho* (a type of armadillo), lizard, and caiman; among
> birds, ostrich, duck, *garza*, and turkey; and every sort of
> fish that fill the streams. Their bread is made from a vari-
> ety of roots: yucca, sweet potato, potato, maize, banana, and
> *zapallo* which is a sort of yucca. Their usual drink is *chicha*
> [. . .] it takes much of the day to cook, stir, and grind up the
> material from which it is made.[22]

There were two types of *chicha*, one for daily use and also a
distilled alcoholic version for ceremonies and festivals.[23] It
was instead the Spanish intruders who often found themselves trapped and isolated by the unexpected floods, blocked
in their movements, with little in the way of supplies to steal
from the abandoned villages. It was not unusual for them to
succumb to hunger.

There was no gold in the great swamp of Llanos; indeed
there were no metals at all except for tin and silver acquired
via trade for making jewelry.[24] The natives produced ele-
mentary manufactured goods: terracotta crockery – plates,
bowls, vases – with simple decorations.[25] The first Spaniards
described them as capable weavers who produced the *tipoy*,
a decorated sort of dress worn by women, and other arti-
cles of clothing. They used cotton and *bibosi*, a fiber obtained
from a variety of ficus, for weaving and also produced mats,

hammocks, and baskets.[26] They were certainly expert in the construction of canoes, their most common means of transport. Their canoes were hollowed out with fire from a single tree trunk and could stretch as long as 18 meters powered by eight to ten oarsmen.[27] The offer of steel hatchets and mauls caught on more quickly among the Indios than did the teaching of the Word. Wood was traditionally used to make tools (a hard shaft for planting, a mortar for grinding maize), but also for bows, arrows, and blowpipes for hunting and fighting, benches for sitting, and musical instruments including a sort of giant flute. They used sharpened animals' teeth and bones as needles for sewing and made shields of woven switches covered in cotton and adorned in feathers to protect them from arrows.[28] Their arrows "in the bloodier wars had six or eight spines pointing backward so that it is horrible to think of extracting them once one has been hit."[29] "Certainly the perfection of these arrows is to be admired, which seem as though prepared for presentation to a king."[30] Their houses were round huts, 3–5 *varas* across (2.5–4.2 meters) built around a central pillar and covered with fronds.[31] "These round huts in which they sleep are better and larger than those of Perú, and the Indios easily install six or eight hammocks, or even more, in each of them."[32] Stone tools like axes were rare, given the complete lack of stone in the Llanos, and could only be acquired through trade with tribes from other regions.

The inhabitants of the Llanos developed interesting methods to reshape the terrain, building straight, raised roads that were protected from flooding and also canals that generally ran parallel to the roads and are still visible today.[33] The canals were built by excavating the material needed to build the roads. If they did not become overgrown, they could be used for part of the dry season as well. The network of canals and raised roads spread over the land of the Mojos and with remarkable concentration in that of the Baures; indeed so thickly as to suggest that they served not only for purposes of communication but perhaps also for ceremonial functions. It is not clear when they were built, and they may date from well before contact. Their high density suggests that the population there may have once been larger than that encountered by the first Europeans; though it might also simply represent accumulation over time by a smaller group.

The material culture of the Llanos fits into the natural framework briefly described above, a description based largely on the observations of the first Europeans to visit the region and especially the Jesuits. Given that those observations date from the time after contact, it is not certain that they accurately describe the situation before the arrival of the Europeans. The first Jesuits, for example, described ornaments made from silver and tin acquired in trade from the Spaniards themselves.[34] Moreover, this description applies to the Mojos and the Baures, not to the other less developed cultures. According to the first visitors, the Baures had a more complex culture than that of the Mojos, as revealed in their clothing (the men occasionally wore a simple tunic while the Mojos were practically naked), their adornments and hairstyles (the women did their hair "like European ladies"[35]), and their huts. The latter were "covered in straw, but with ability and proportion between the patio and the large rooms in which they lived, and were clean and spacious, care that distinguished them from other heathens; not to mention the way in which they decorated their walls with mats woven in interesting ways."[36] The Mojos were simpler: "Their huts were built of wood and straw; they ate sitting on the ground and slept in hammocks or on mats on the ground; their only protection from the cold – even when they were rocked by fever – was fire."[37] Some of the Baures villages were surrounded by pikes and defensive canals, and the evidence of earthworks – canals, roads, and mounds for agriculture – are denser and more widespread than among the Mojos.

It is impossible to know the size of the Llanos population when the Spaniards first arrived. Significant contact began in the middle of the seventeenth century but for over a century was sporadic and limited to the edges of the vast plain. In that initial period there were a number of expeditions and raids to capture men and women. The less remote Indios also traded with the Spaniards of Santa Cruz – which suggests more or less regular interaction – before the Jesuits began their evangelical work in the last third of the century. A population estimate based on reliable observation can only be made for this later period, and any attempt to project backward in time is risky. William Denevan, author of the first complete cultural geography of the region, estimates that the population at the end of the seventeenth century amounted to about 100,000, but that this figure was well below that of a century before; for the end of the sixteenth century he suggests a figure of 200–500,000.[38] This estimate, however, is not based on data, but on the conviction that the decline of the indigenous population – which certainly occurred in most of the continent following the arrival of the Europeans – was everywhere violent and the product in particular, if not exclusively, of the importation of European pathogens (smallpox, measles, and typhus) that wiped out the non-immunized natives. In its most radical form, this "epidemiological" paradigm hypothesizes a population decline of 90–95 percent compared to pre-Columbian, or pre-contact, levels.[39]

Historical research has confirmed that indigenous Americans did experience demographic collapse. It has also demonstrated that the scale of that collapse varied according to region, environmental conditions, the organization and density of the population, and the degree of social and economic disruption caused by the Conquest. For the Mojos, in fact, we really don't possess any evidence that the population at the end of the seventeenth century was much smaller than it had been at the time of contact. We do know that smallpox spread through much of South America around 1590, and there is testimony regarding its disastrous impact on the Indios of Santa Cruz.[40] Yet smallpox, like the other diseases responsible for high indigenous mortality, is spread by contact and so favored by high levels of mobility, trade, and population density. The populations of the Llanos instead were isolated and dispersed over a vast territory in small settlements; and we don't know to what degree they were affected by the epidemic, if at all. Moreover, the damp climate of the Llanos does not favor "face to face" transmission of the virus. Any population estimate for the mid-sixteenth century then can only be conjecture and based on an examination of the material culture of the Llanos ethnicities and the productive potential of the territory, factors that suggest a low population density.

We can locate a first clue to understanding the demographic context of the Llanos in settlement patterns. The villages were certainly small, consisting for the most part of a few dozen dwellings. Altamirano pointed out that it was impossible to have large villages in a territory where the limited cultivable land was surrounded by "a sea of water" in the flooding season.[41] In addition, the varying course of the rivers – along which the villages were situated – required frequent moves, an operation that becomes more difficult as villages become larger. We can derive some information from the testimony of survivors of the 1617 expedition led by Solís de Holguín into the land of the Mojos and given twenty years later to the president of the Audiencia de Charcas (the highest authority in Alto Perú).[42] That expedition, like many others, included among its goals the capture

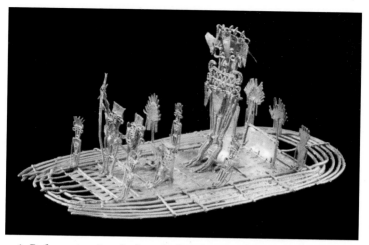

1 *Raft representing the legend of El Dorado, Muisca, 700–1600* CE
(Pasca, Cundinamarca)

2 *Anthropomorphic chest-plate, Sinú, 200–1000* CE

3 *Anthropomorphic chest-plate, Tolima, 0–1000* CE *(Quimbaya, Quindío)*

4 *Head of a club with animal figure, Sinú, 200–1000* CE *(Moñitos, Córdoba)*

5 *Man wearing a bat mask, Tairona, 600–1600* CE *(Rio Palomino)*

6 *Ritual mask, Calima, 300 BCE–1200* CE *(Restrepo, Valle del Cauca)*

7 *Chest-plate, Quimbaya 1000–1600* CE *(Caicedonia, Valle del Cauca)*

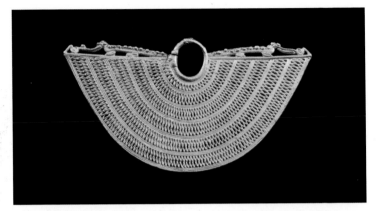

8 Earring of soldered filigree, Sinú, 200–1600 CE *(Córdoba)*

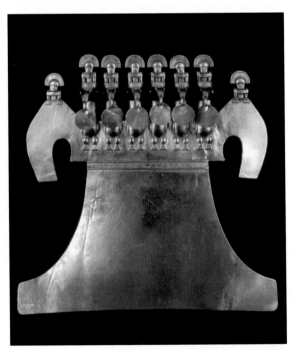

9 Chest-plate with anthropomorphic figures, Muisca, 700–1600 CE
(Guatavita, Cundinamarca)

10–11 Various ways to cross the streams: horses, cattle, carts, and the missionaries themselves

12 *An Indian battle; two warriors in the foreground are wearing protective tunics*

13–14 The capturing of wild horses with boleadoras *(above) and of cattle with lassoes (below)*

15 *The use of horses in war and peace*

16–17 *The preparation and drinking of* chicha; *drunkenness and dancing*

18 The harvest and threshing of grain and plowing of the fields

19 The gathering of honey

20 Women capturing grasshoppers – which the Indios eat – and preparing dried meat

21 Children playing and diving into the river

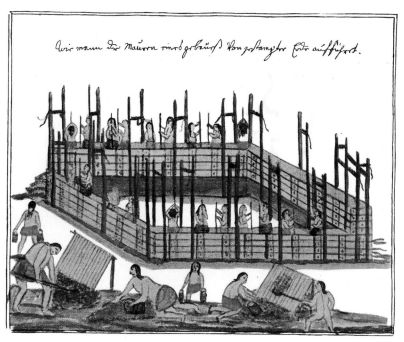

22 The construction of a building

23 A horse race

24 *Celebration in honor of the king of Spain*

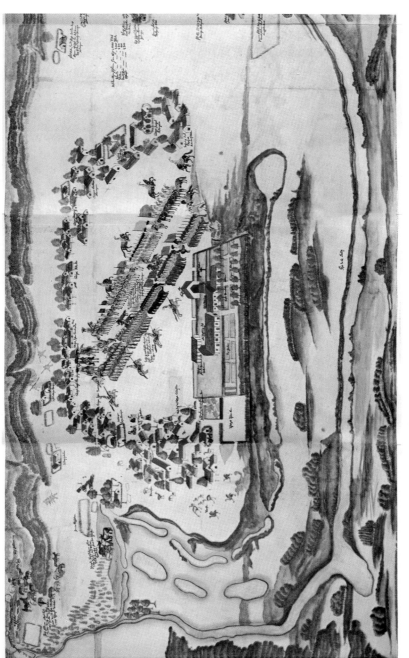

25 *Panorama of the San Javier Mission and the surrounding fields*

26 *The San Javier Mission*

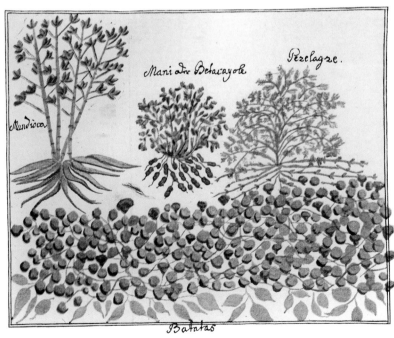

27 *Tubers and roots formed the basis of the Indian diet: sweet potatoes, maní, cassava*

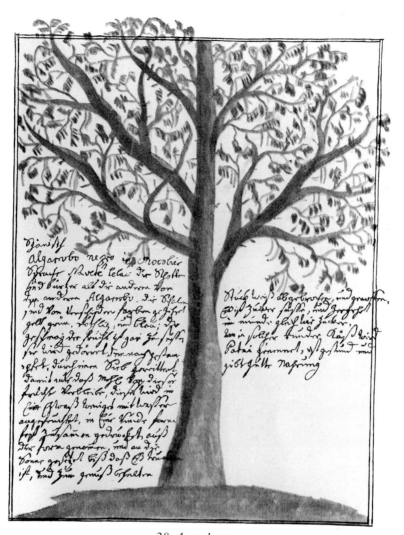

28 *A carob tree*

29 *Types of palms*

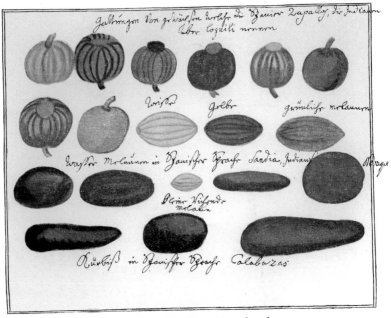

30 *Varieties of squash and melon*

31 Aquatic birds

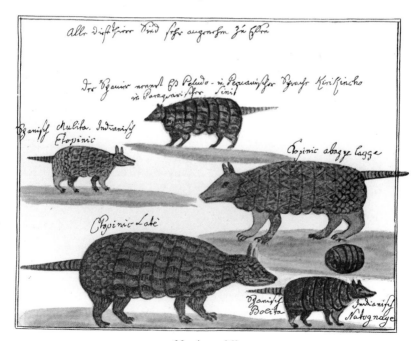

32 Armadillos

33 *Birds of prey, gulls, owls*

34 *The capybara, a large aquatic mammal*

of natives for their labor. The locals figured this out soon enough and responded by fleeing, a more effective defense than the taking up of arms. The memories of brief observations recorded in these declarations constitute pretty thin documentary evidence, but it is the best we have. We should also keep in mind that they probably tend to exaggeration, given the myth of gold and the search for large and wealthy populations just beyond the horizon. The investigation also includes testimony of several Indios from the Tapacuras, a tribe that had good relations with the Spaniards and a direct and conflictual one with the Torocosis (another tribe of the Mojos). These Indios stated that their province consisted of forty-four villages, one of which counted 700 inhabitants, another more or less 100, and most about 300.[43] Among the members of the expedition, that first stopped among the friendly Tapacuras before proceeding 7 or 8 leagues into enemy territory, the testimony of Captain Gregorio Jiménez is especially interesting; he had lived in Santa Cruz for thirty years. According to Jiménez, one detachment encountered four partly abandoned villages on either side of a one-league stretch of river. They had also seen a large field with 500 maize depositaries, "that constitute their granaries,"[44] as well as a smaller field. Others who went further encountered eleven villages, while the prisoners taken said there were twenty. These prisoners consisted of fifty women and a few men (probably those who were slowest to flee) who had been taken, according to the discreet narrator, "in order that they should learn the language." Jiménez added, with an eye to future expeditions, that there were enough resources in the land of the Mojos "to support an expedition of 300 men for a year" (the expedition of Holguín consisted of seventy-five Spaniards and 200 Indio auxiliaries).[45] According to Sergeant Bartolomé de Heredia who was also part of the detachment, they encountered one village with 280 dwellings and, having traveled for one league, he estimated that there were 3,000 Indios.[46] Perhaps the most interesting testimony is that of Juan de Limpias: Holguín's expedition, once it had entered into the land of the Mojos, encountered resistance and one of their Indios was killed, but the Mojo warriors had to retreat "because the Spaniards killed fourteen or fifteen men, both from horseback and with their harquebuses."[47] Holguín then sent an exploratory detachment of twenty men, including Juan de Limpias (and later mentioned by other witnesses as well). De Limpias estimated there were 3,000 people in the region explored, divided as follows:

- one large village of 400 dwellings, ninety kitchens (covered enclosures for communal food preparation), and nine *bebederos* (communal areas for ceremonies and festivals);
- another nine smaller villages consisting of a few huts, between ten and thirty.

In the course of their exploration, they found two large communal fields: the first included 700 food depositories ("maize and other legumes") and the second 500; "judging from appearance, each depositary contained between 20 and 30 *fanegas* of food." Assuming these observations were correct and calculating only for maize (ears, not kernels), we can estimate that these depositaries could have fed a population of between 1,000 and 1,500 for a year.[48] Another witness, Antonio Justiniano, spoke of seven or eight villages, while Francisco Sanchez Gregorio counted seven villages, the largest of which contained 350 dwellings, fifty kitchens, and twenty *bebederos*. According to the Mojos, instead, there were thirty-six *caciques*.[49]

There is a certain consistency to these testimonies. The expedition only got part way into the land of the Mojos; it encountered a number of villages (up to a maximum of eleven according to the various accounts), usually with a few dozen inhabitants and in the largest case with a few hundred. The captured Indios spoke of twenty villages and there was also a reference to thirty-six *caciques* (probably village heads). The older Tapacura Indios, who had lived their entire lives near the Mojos, referred to forty-four villages and an average size of 300. The expedition killed many Indios and took several dozen prisoners (mostly women); and many of the villages visited were semi-abandoned. The scale of agriculture encountered and the stored harvests suggest a population size compatible with these other reports. Taking into account the nature of the expedition, that the reports were made twenty years after the fact, that the purpose had never been to count or quantify, and that we are looking for an order of magnitude, not a precise figure, it seems reasonable to place a maximum estimate on the population in the range of 12–15,000.

For more precise ideas regarding the demographic dimensions of the Mojos, we have to wait till the mid-1670s when the Jesuits began their evangelical campaign, a campaign that culminated in the founding of the first mission in 1682. In particular, we owe our early general understanding of the region to the Fathers José del Castillo, Pedro Marbán, and Cipriano Barace who during their stay in the region traversed it numerous times. The Jesuit leadership of Perú was especially interested in the characteristics of the region, the size of the population, and the feasibility of conversion. The missionaries (*operarios*) were few, and there was little interest in devoting precious resources to projects that stood scant chance of success. The three Fathers' first report in 1676 did not satisfy the provincial Father who asked for a supplemental study. That study, also from 1676 and signed by José del Castillo, is a fundamental source for our anthropological and cultural understanding of the region.[50] It includes a wealth of detail on the location and size of settlements. Del Castillo visited and identified thirty-two villages with an average population of sixty-six (corresponding to a total population of 2,120). The two largest villages each contained a couple of hundred people. Another nine were listed, but without population details. On the basis of the information gathered, José del Castillo counted 6,000 inhabitants in seventy villages.[51]

The superiors in Lima wanted to know more, and a little while later Fathers Marbán, Barace, and Clemente Ygarza organized a four-month expedition that explored the upper stretch of the Mamoré (the most densely populated area of the Mojos), following the course of the river and its vicinity over two degrees of latitude (about 220 kilometers). They recorded the names, populations, and locations of fifty-eight villages comprising 3,600 Indios (plus six other villages that they did not see but about which they had reports). In terms of size, these included four villages with fewer than 20 inhabitants, nineteen with 20–40, thirteen with 40–60, ten with 60–80, four with 80–100, five with 100–120, and three with over 120. For the most part these were *pueblecitos* with an average population of 60 (twelve to fifteen families) splintered among twenty-two different named clans or ethnicities. Leandro Tormo Sanz succeeded in mapping the area visited by the three Jesuits; it covered 17,600 square kilometers corresponding to a density of 0.21 inhabitants per square kilometer. They had, however, been unable to visit all the villages of which they had heard and so Tormo Sanz guessed that the population density lay instead between 0.3 and 0.4 (5,280–7,040 inhabitants).[52] David Block accepts this estimate but has taken it further. He imagines that all the area around the major rivers had a similar density: not just the upper Mamoré and its tributaries where the Mojos lived, but also other regions like that near the Iténez and San Miguel rivers inhabited by the Baures, the other major ethnicity. In

Table 2.1: Estimates of the aboriginal population of Mojos at the beginning of the missionary period, c.1680

Ecological region	Area (km²)	Hypothetical density (persons/km²)		Population estimate	
		minimum	maximum	minimum	maximum
Major river network	27,000	0.315	0.42	8,500	11,000
Interfluvial zone	153,000	0.08	0.11	12,240	16,830
Total	180,000			20,740	27,830

Source: David Block, "In Search of El Dorado. Spanish Entry into Moxos, A Tropical Frontier, 1550–1767," PhD diss., Austin: The University of Texas at Austin, 1980, p. 52. For the relevant hypotheses, based on the work of Tormo Sanz, see the text.

that way, for an area of 27,000 kilometers he gets a population of 8,500–11,000. For the remaining 85 percent of the territory (153,000 square kilometers), the areas between the rivers consisting mostly of pampas and savannah where the environmental conditions were less favorable and the population more dispersed, he estimates a density one *quarter* of that along the rivers and so comes up with a total population for the Llanos in 1680 between 21,000 and 28,000 (see table 2.1).[53] The series of hypotheses used to arrive at this estimate is long, but the reasoning is sound. Many witnesses referred to small villages spread over the territory "every two leagues or more."[54] If "every two leagues or more" means 3 leagues on average (15 kilometers), then we would have one village every 225 square kilometers; if we apply this density to the 27,000 square kilometers of settled riverine area (as defined by Block), then we get 120 villages. Assuming 100–200 inhabitants per village, we get a total population of 12,000–24,000, an order of magnitude compatible with Block's estimate. We need not push this exercise any further, as every adjustment of our hypotheses – entirely legitimate given the approximate nature of the data – will give us different results.

In 1682, as already mentioned, the first Jesuit mission was founded. The work of conversion and reorganization of the Llanos continued for the next several decades at the end of which the reality encountered by the first Fathers in the 1670s, probably not much different from that which had existed prior to contact, was profoundly changed.

The reports and other documents from the late seventeenth century and the beginning of the eighteenth century describe a situation already experiencing strong forces of change. Nonetheless, and for the sake of completeness, we should include some further notes on the areas that were to undergo conversion at the beginning of that process.

According to the first missionaries actually stationed in the zone, the Mojos "numbered 4,000 souls divided among fifty villages, each independent of the other" (eighty inhabitants per village).[55] Those first three missionaries lived "in a village of twelve dwellings protected by a thick and impenetrable forest." In the foundation phase of the missions, Fathers Orellana and de la Vega baptized the infidels in three villages "that numbered over 700 souls."[56] Among the Baures, there were 124 villages "with few inhabitants as is the custom among the infidels," though they were enough for twenty "reductions" of 2,000 Indios each (which suggests the villages averaged over 300). The same author affirms that nonetheless it was difficult to group Indios into the classic reductions "because in order to gather together 3,000 souls, it might be necessary to combine twenty different villages spread over twenty leagues," which implies instead villages of 150 Indios.[57] In the region inhabited by the Movimas, a relatively barbarous tribe that lived between the Mamoré and Beni rivers, there were presumably 20,000 Indios divided among eighty villages (250 per village).[58] On the edge of the Llanos, the attempt to convert the Canisianas did not go well; there were 4–5,000 of them divided into seventy-two villages (sixty to seventy people per village).[59] The Itonomas, another primitive tribe that lived on the edge of the savannah between the Mojos and the Baures, numbered 6,000 divided into twenty-three villages (261 per village).[60]

The villages then were small and consisted of at most a few hundred Indios and usually a few dozen. Those dimensions were compatible with a subsistence regime that depended primarily on hunting and fishing and on farming restricted to areas protected from flooding; with a social structure that lacked complex stratification; and with a rudimentary level of technology.

The difficult passage between Cuzco and Cochabamba – the closest Spanish city to the heart of the Llanos – crosses over the Andean Cordillera whose peaks of 7,000 meters are interspersed with passes of 4,000 meters. Beyond this barrier stretched the land of the Paititi or the Grand Mojo from where there arrived the *Gran Noticia* of an El Dorado that had eluded Quesada, Gonzalo Pizarro, Pedro de Candía, and many others easily given to fantasy if strong of temperament. For over a century their followers tried to climb over or skirt around that barrier and penetrate the mysterious region beyond in search first of gold, then of labor, and finally of souls. Yet beyond the Andes there was neither gold, nor silver, nor iron, nor even stone. For much of the year there was just a great swamp.

III

THE MYTH OF PAITITI, FATHER-TIGER, AND
THE MYSTERIOUS INCAN MIGRATIONS OVER
THE ANDES. A RICH AND NOBLE MESTIZO
WITH FOURTEEN MEN SEEKS TO CONQUER
HALF OF AMERICA. EL DORADO BOGS
DOWN IN THE SWAMPS OF THE MOJOS.
THE CITIZENS OF SANTA CRUZ – ELEVEN
DISORDERLY STREETS – LOOK FOR SLAVES.

In 1635 Captain Gregorio Jiménez, a veteran of exploration beyond the Andes, observed:

> My conclusion, confirmed by men who know these lands, is that [. . .] this «*Noticia*», which has been repeated over and over for many years [and has been the driving force behind] explorations undertaken in many places by many different captains and has been called by many different names – Paititi in Paraguay, Mojos in Perú, El Dorado in the Nuevo Reino [de Granada, today Colombia] – refers always to the same thing: in Paraguay they look for it to the west; in Perú

they look for it in the east; while in this city [Santa Cruz de la Sierra] they look to the north; and in the Nuevo Reino they look to the south.[1]

This statement came more than a century after the fall of the Incan empire. All of South America was firmly in the hands of the Spanish and the Portuguese, who numbered at least half a million by then and had explored, traveled, and traded throughout the continent, founding its major cities. And yet no one really knew what lay beyond the Andes in the regions of the Amazon basin, the Orinoco, and the upper Paraguay; save for a few rapid forays by intrepid adventurers, these lands were largely unexplored. The *Gran Noticia* of fabulous riches waiting to be discovered there was still alive. The president of the Audiencia de Charcas (Alto Perú), Juan de Lizarazu, in fact asked Philip IV (in a letter dated 1 March, 1636) for authorization to leave his post and undertake an expedition across the Andes to the land of the Mojos, claiming: "The pacification and conquest of that province is much talked about here, as in addition to the infinite number of Indios that reside there, one hears incredible reports of large deposits of gold and silver."[2] In support of that request, Lizarazu had gathered a large number of testimonies (to which we referred in chapter II, including that of Gregorio Jiménez) and had found a financier for the undertaking: "an *hidalgo* named Pedro de Iriarte who has offered in a public document (a copy of which I send to Your Majesty) 54 thousand pesos," so that the expedition could be accomplished "at no cost to the royal coffers."[3] The request was turned down and the expedition did not take place; the Audiencia could not spare its president.

In fact, the expeditions to the Llanos undertaken up to that time had already revealed the real situation there: a sparse and simple population and an absence of wealth. Yet the hope remained that those riches lay "beyond" the plain, in the great Amazon forests or in the rugged and unexplored Brazilian *chapadas* of Mato Grosso. And that hope was enough to convince the authorities to issue licenses for exploration and to inspire soldiers and adventurers to take part in them. It is unclear whether Lizarazu really thought he would find gold and treasure; though it does appear that he aspired to become governor of the region (as he requested of the king).

A century separates these projects of the mid-seventeenth century from those of Candía and Peranzures (see chapter I), the expeditions across the Andes in search of El Dorado that probed furthest to the south. To better understand the later period, we need to trace the origins of the myth of Paititi or the Grand Mojo, the southern version of El Dorado. Then we can follow the Spanish attempts to penetrate the Llanos and other nearby regions. Some of these followed the traditional route, climbing over the Cordillera to travel the 800 kilometers that separate Cuzco from Cochabamba, the closest Spanish settlement, as the crow flies, to the center of the Llanos. Others instead came from the east, making their way up the Paraguay river till near the Llanos, the heart of which lay 1,400 kilometers from Asunción. And others still left from Santa Cruz de la Sierra, Perú's southern outpost and the point of access for the Jesuits in the late seventeenth century.

The origins of the Grand Mojo-Paititi legend are obscure (Pai-Titi or Father-Tiger according to the philologist Jiménez de la Espada),[4] but Garcilaso de la Vega offers a remarkable and imaginative explanation that some believe may have a bit of truth in it. According to Garcilaso (in book VI, chapter XIII, of the *Comentarios*), Yupanqui, tenth king of the Incas, sought to expand his empire to the east, beyond the Andes:[5]

He had heard that one of the best of the inhabited provinces was what the Indians called Musu and the Spaniards
Los Mojos, which could be entered by a great river running
through the Antis to the east of the city [Cuzco]. It consists
of many rivers that flow together at this point. There are
five main courses each with a different name [. . .] all of
which form a very great river called Amarumayu.[6]

According to this account, Yupanqui and his men subdued
the riverine populations of the Chunchu (a generic term
used by the Incas for the independent and "barbarian" tribes
to the east of the Andes), and then "advanced and reduced
many other tribes, until they reached the Province called
Musu, a region peopled by a great many war-like people and
of great natural fertility. It is said to be two hundred leagues
from the city of Cuzco." The expedition seems to have been
welcomed and:

they boldly persuaded the Musus to submit and serve the
Inca, child of the Sun whom his father had sent from heaven
to teach men to live like men and not like beasts, and to worship the Sun as their god and give up the adoration of animals,
and sticks and stones, and other unworthy objects. And finding that the Musus listened to them willingly, the Incas gave
them a fuller account of their laws, privileges, and customs,
and told them of the great deeds performed by their kings in
past conquests, and how many provinces they had subdued,
mentioning that many had submitted of their own accord,
beseeching the Incas to receive them as vassals, and that they
worshipped the Incas as gods [. . .] All this astonished the
Musus, who were delighted to receive the friendship of the
Incas and to embrace their idolatry, laws, and customs, which
they thought good, promising to be governed by them and
to worship the Sun as their chief god. They did not wish to

admit vassalage, because the Inca had not conquered them and subjected them by force of arms. They were, however, delighted to be his friends and confederates [. . .] By virtue of this friendship the Musus let the Incas settle in their country. There were little more than a thousand left when they arrived, for the rest had perished in the wars and amidst the hardships of the journey. The Musus gave them their daughters in marriage and were delighted to intermarry with them. Even today they hold the Incas in great veneration and are governed by them in peace and war.

Subsequently, Musu ambassadors went to Cuzco to render homage to the Incas, and "[t]his league and friendship lasted until the arrival of the Spaniards and their conquest of Peru."[7] Garcilaso himself doubted this account – "some of these deeds seem to me incredible"[8] – but observed that a number of Spanish expeditions beyond the Andes had gathered rumors and testimony that might have confirmed this earlier story. Another historian of the Conquest, Sarmento de Gamboa, also referred to a similar story.[9]

Others have believed the claims of Father Diego Felipe de Alcaya who repeated the stories told to him by his father. According to that account, it was Manco Inca, a nephew of Huayna Cápac (the father of Atahuallpa), who was given the charge of colonizing the barbarous peoples across the Andes. After much wandering, he crossed the Llanos and colonized the Sierra de Parecis (today part of the Brazilian province of Rondônia that borders on Bolivia). This settlement maintained its isolation because of the protection offered by the Guaporé, Mamoré, and Madeira rivers (see map 6) and so fed the legend of a rich and civilized people living in the interior beyond the Llanos.[10]

It would require volumes to sort out the web of legends, rumors, testimonies, documents, and real and imagined facts

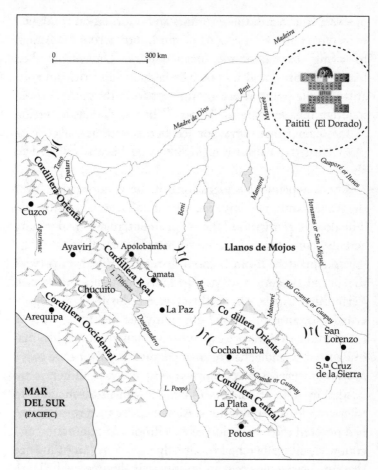

*6 The arrows indicate the entry routes to Llanos de Mojos from Perú;
above, the region of Paititi*

related to Paititi. We can perhaps sum it up as follows: the
Incas expanded to the east, occasionally crossing over the
Andes, but only in a few cases did that expansion lead to true
colonization; the Spaniards gathered rumors and information about expeditions (like that of Yupanqui) that settled
near the Llanos (though "near" understood in the context

of a vast continent); these rumors and information combined with others about an exodus of the Indios across the Andes, following the fall of the Incan empire. The legend then located Paititi – and its possibly fabulous and rich inhabitants – at the point where great rivers from the Andes flowed together into an immense lagoon.[11] In a less fantastic version of the legend that corresponded better with actual geography, Paititi lay in the rugged Sierra de Parecis referred to above.

The independent explorations of the conquistadors over the Andes continued until the arrival of Viceroy Francisco de Toledo who reorganized the government, relaunched mining activity, concentrated dispersed populations, eliminated the last independent Incan holdout in remote Vilcabamba (with the brutal execution of young Tupac Amaru), and turned Perú into a true colony in the service of Spain. Toledo governed with an iron fist and efficiently; he had little patience for anarchic exploratory expeditions. Many of these, like that of Pedro de Candía, had been encouraged by the desire of *pro tempore* governors to distance potential rivals. Others were headed by difficult and ambitious individuals, disinclined to tolerate rules and limitations. Already in 1550, a royal decree had ordered the suspension of expeditions of exploration and conquest, either planned or already underway; an ordinance that was circumvented and ultimately ineffective.[12] With regard to the Mojos, Philip II issued another ordinance in 1573 assigning the right to *descubrimiento* of that region to the Spaniards of Santa Cruz de la Sierra (founded twelve years before).[13] A letter written to Philip II in 1577 testifies to Toledo's aversion for these sorts of expedition. In it Toledo denounces the criteria used to authorize and conduct them: the *descubridores* oppress the Indios with tyranny and cruelty; they overlook their obligation to impart religious instruction; they inspire revolts; they are themselves actors and instigators in conflicts with other Spaniards; and as often as not the outcome of their expeditions is disastrous.[14] Centralizer that he was, Toledo had little sympathy for high-risk and anarchic enterprises that often ended up costing the state, in spite of the principle, largely ignored, according to which these undertakings were to be financed by their organizers.

Just the same, there were many attempts in the 1560s to penetrate into the unknown regions of Chunchos and Mojos, following the leads of Candía and Peranzures. These expeditions crossed the Cordillera 30 leagues east of Cuzco by way of Opatari (Pedro de Candía's route) and worked their way down the Manu river; or else they crossed the Carabaya Cordillera by way of Sandia and San Juan del Oro (where gold had in fact been discovered), 30 leagues south of Opatari, following the valleys and tributaries of the Madre de Dios; or else still farther south, east of Lake Titicaca via Camata and following the tributaries of the upper Beni. A still more southern access point to the Llanos lay east of Cochabamba, following down the valleys of the tributaries to the Mamoré (see map 6).

All of these routes, however, were extremely difficult given the height of the mountains and passes (over 4,000 meters and so causing the *soroche* or altitude sickness); the rocky, treacherous descents; and the need to navigate rivers that tumbled down the steep eastern slopes of the Andes. A document from 1570 lists the *entradas* of the previous decade almost all of which ended disastrously.[15] In 1561, the Viceroy Conde de Nieva entrusted Gómez de Tordoya with an expedition along the Tono river for the purpose of establishing a *gobernación*; but he quickly rescinded the authorization. It was instead assigned at the end of the same year to Juan Nieto who crossed over at Camata and returned three months later with little to show for his effort. The next year, Antón de Gastos's expedition left from Cochabamba and accomplished little more. In 1563, Diego Alemán set out to the Mojos from Cochabamba but his expedition was wiped out by Indios. The same fate awaited the expedition of Lujan that left, again from Cochabamba, in search of gold mines; he and eight companions were killed. The 1569 expedition of Cuéllar and Ortega, consisting of seventy Spaniards, was instead cancelled because of lack of authorization.

The best known of these attempts is that of Juan Álvarez Maldonado, illegitimate son of a Salamanca *hidalgo* and himself a wealthy resident of Cuzco. The Viceroy Lope García de Castro gave him authorization to "discover" a region that was theoretically vast and promised him the *gobernación* and attendant privileges should he be successful. The area assigned to him by the royal bureaucrats covered five full degrees of latitude – 500 kilometers – and 3,000 kilometers of longitude, all the way to the coast of Brazil between Salvador de Bahia and Rio de Janeiro; it made up a rectangle of 1.5 million square kilometers – more than France, Spain, and Italy taken together – with an eastern border that extended beyond the "line of Tordesillas" that in 1498 had divided the continent between Spain and Portugal. Maldonado planned to call this vast territory Nueva Andalucía and to conquer it with just the fourteen Spaniards he took along with him (in addition to the usual Indian auxiliaries). However, after he crossed over the Cordillera and arrived at the Madre de Dios, he realized he needed more men and so returned to Cuzco to recruit another 100. He had a fleet of canoes and *balsas* built, and on 20 May, 1568, it departed under the command of Captain Escobar to begin the voyage to the land of Paititi and the Mojos, with Spaniards, Indios, horses, arms, and provisions all on board. Escobar and his men reached the lower course of the river near the confluence with the Beni and encountered Indios who were friendly at first but then became hostile and wiped them out. In the meantime, Maldonado, who knew nothing of Escobar's fate, had gathered another 120 men in Cuzco and begun sailing down the river. But it was November by then, the rainy season had begun, and the churning river created a thousand difficulties for the recently initiated sailors. Having learned finally of Escobar's disaster, the survivors left the river and in a miserable state emerged from the forest well south of Cuzco at San Juan del Oro in the province of Carabaya.[16] Garcilaso added his own picturesque note. According to his account, Maldonado and two of his companions, a monk and Simon the master blacksmith, were captured by Indios. Maldonado was freed immediately, but the other two were held for some time and, during their imprisonment, Simon was forced to forge hatchets and axes for the Indios. Having saved their skins, the monk and the smith re-emerged from the wilderness two years later and described their wanderings.[17] The spirited Maldonado, who had more enthusiasm than brains, wrote a report on the expedition for Viceroy Toledo and asked that he authorize a new undertaking. The request was denied. According to Maldonado, beyond the river and plain they had explored:

> There is a cordillera of snowy mountains which according to the Indios who have seen it resembles that of Perú [. . .] They say that this sierra is rich in metals and filled with people, much as in Perú, and they perform the same ceremonies, wear the same clothes, and raise the same animals; and they say that the Indios of Perú come from there [. . .] And they say that the greatest wealth of all America lies there. In the province of Paititi there are mines of gold and silver and a huge quantity of amber as well.[18]

Toledo was unconvinced. In a letter to Philip II, he mentions having refused to authorize the expedition. He also informs the king that he has used Maldonado – "who has served and labored well" – in the destruction of the Incan holdout at Vilcabamba, the operation that ended with the death of Tupac Amaru. But he adds:

> I do not believe he is the type to send into unexplored regions on his own. And so I prefer to limit him to the small place that he began to establish at the beginning of his voyage. There with a small number of followers he can call upon the Indios of the district to come in peace so that they may receive the doctrine of the apostles.[19]

In spite of its failure, Maldonado's effort refocused attention on the myth of Paititi; it also demonstrates clearly the huge gap between ambition and hope on the one hand – foundation of a "Reyno de la Nueva Andalucía" – and the reality of the situation on the other: the lack of resources and (especially) knowledge and the enormous natural and political obstacles to overcome. A rational individual like Toledo saw through the emptiness of these initiatives. Meanwhile there were new developments, namely the discovery of a route to the region of the Mojos that did not cross over the Andes but instead originated in the remote basin of the Rio de la Plata, a relatively easy path, but one that crossed swampy, desolate, and sparsely inhabited lands along the course of the upper Paraguay river.

In 1558, ten years prior to Maldonado's expedition, Asunción was a Spanish city, an Episcopal seat, and capital of the Rio de la Plata *gobernación*. It had been founded twenty years earlier on the high banks of a bend in the Paraguay river, 100 kilometers north of its confluence with the Paraná and 1,000 kilometers from the Rio de la Plata estuary. Asunción then was the major center of Spanish colonization for the immense region that includes present-day

Argentina, Uruguay, and Paraguay. Its importance though should not deceive us; it was a modest town consisting of a few stone buildings – perhaps the *cabildo*, the cathedral, and the home of the governor. The simple homes of its few colonists were instead built of mud bricks and covered in palm fronds; while the quarters of the Spaniards' Indian servants lay close at hand. Around 1570, Juan López de Velasco, the royal cosmographer, counted 300 families of Spaniards in Asunción (*vecinos*) and 2–3,000 *mestizos*.[20] The expedition of Ñuflo de Chaves, who himself hailed from Estremadura, must then have impressed the town's inhabitants as they lined up along the *embarcadero* to watch its departure. It consisted of 150 Spaniards and 1,500–2,000 Indian auxiliaries loaded onto twenty or so brigantines and a large number of *balsas* and canoes.[21] The Spanish population of the city was about 2,000, so 150 men represented a considerable human investment. Officially the expedition was directed to populate the land of the Xarayes, a Guaraní tribe that lived on the banks of the Paraguay 800 kilometers upstream from Asunción, though it is likely that Chaves had grander plans of exploration and conquest.

Nor did this 1558 expedition represent the first attempt on the part of the Spaniards of Rio de la Plata to explore the north-west in hopes of finding a way through to Perú; Ñuflo de Chaves himself had taken part in an earlier expedition commanded by Irala, the colony's strongman for the twenty years following the founding of Asunción. His aim had been to make contact with the wealthy lands of Perú and so establish a possible outlet for the small and isolated province of Rio de la Plata. This earlier expedition had headed up the Paraguay and plunged into the Chaco where Irala and company found it impossible to proceed. Chaves was given the mission of continuing on to Perú with a small delegation to President la Gasca. Chaves made it to Lima and was well received by la Gasca, who was busy at the time with putting down the rebellion led by Gonzalo Pizarro. La Gasca promised aid to the Rio de la Plata colony, but on condition that those colonists stay within their own territory and not involve themselves in the affairs of Perú. Engaged in a full-scale civil war, la Gasca did not want the arrival of other ambitious adventurers to further complicate the situation in his domain.[22] By 1558, Chaves may have imagined that with Perú pacified his earlier ambitions could be realized, namely the establishment of a province that could act as a transit route between the Mar del Nord and Perú and so create opportunities for power and wealth.

Chaves's expedition was full of interesting adventures that could easily sidetrack our narrative if we let them. Working its way up the Paraguay, the expedition experienced its share of accidents and mishaps. It did arrive in the land of the Xarayes, located at around 17° latitude, though it was a swampy land that suffered flooding and so was a poor site for establishment of a settlement.[23] The Indios there confirmed the existence of rich lands to the north; they probably meant Perú, but Chaves and his men interpreted their description as a confirmation of the existence of Paititi and the Grand Mojo, presumably to motivate the troops. Chaves continued to navigate northward for a few dozen kilometers and then turned to the west in what is today the extreme eastern edge of Bolivia. There they entered into the land of the Chiquitos (so-called because they lived in little huts with low entrances) who proved to be fairly hostile; there are confused reports of a battle centered on a fortification with palisades in which the Spaniards lost sixteen men (one imagines the indigenous losses were some multiple of that).[24] The Chiquitos apparently used poisoned arrows. A notary public accompanied Chaves and kept track of the ordinances and decrees issued by the expedition leader. A document dated 10 May, 1559, makes reference to these events and includes provisions that for the time would have been considered "humanitarian:" Chaves instructed that no Indios below the age of twelve or over forty be captured, and those who were taken would be freed once the expedition made it to its (still indeterminate) destination.[25] Adversity discouraged many of Chaves's companions, and about half decided to return to Asunción. Chaves himself pushed ahead and on 1 August, 1559, officially founded Nueva Asunción on the banks of the Guapay river, though it turned out to be little more than an encampment and was quickly abandoned in spite of the official seal. While the difficulties Chaves encountered up to that point – natural obstacles, long distances, hostile Indios – were of the usual sort, those that followed and from which Chaves emerged victorious would have to be called political. As soon as Nueva Asunción had been founded, his men encountered members of another expedition, that of Andrés Manso. Manso had received a license from the Viceroy Marques de Cañete to discover the "Mojos," while Chaves's authorization (issued by the governor of Asunción) was of lower rank and was limited to settlement among the Xarayes. Chaves defused the potential conflict and came to an agreement with Manso by offering to go to Lima with one of the latter's trusted aides in order to find a solution. Apparently Chaves and the viceroy had family ties, and Chaves was in any case an affable and persuasive man and much experienced. He had ably negotiated in Lima at the time of la Gasca and managed to gain the confidence of Cañete as well. At the end of 1559, Chaves and Manso's emissary were in Lima. Convinced by the arguments of Chaves, the viceroy issued an ordinance creating the province of Mojos and appointed Chaves as its "lieutenant" governor (a post initially assigned to Cañete's son, though he never actually assumed it). Manso was instead relegated to an area that included the warlike Chiriguanos. It was a triumph for Chaves who returned to Nueva Asunción with Peruvian reinforcements and on 26 February, 1561, founded Santa Cruz de la Sierra (though in fact the city changed both in name – it was also called San Lorenzo de la Frontera and La Barranca – and location, being moved several times between its foundation and 1620). Shortly after its foundation, the city received new colonists from Asunción and from Perú and became a viable settlement.

Although Santa Cruz de la Sierra is today a bustling metropolis of 1.5 million people, the second largest in Bolivia and economically the most dynamic, for centuries it was the modest south-eastern outpost of the Viceroyalty of Perú. In 1788, Viedma described it as a minor center with 10,627 inhabitants – of whom 4,303 were Spaniards – and eleven roads "with neither form nor order," a central plaza, a modest cathedral, and adobe dwellings "covered with fronds from a palm called *motacú*." According to Viedma: "The main houses are in the center of the city; their walls are of adobe; some are roofed in tile, others with concave tiles carved out of palm wood."[26] The foundation of Santa Cruz de la Sierra changes the course of our story. The ordinance of 1573 (later reconfirmed) gave the inhabitants of that settlement the rights to exploration and conquest in the land of the Mojos, namely that presumed but ever more elusive El Dorado. Santa Cruz lies near the Guapay river which allows easy navigation northward into the Llanos. No longer did explorers have to scale the Andes or cross dense forests in order to reach the heart of the land of the Mojos.

The city of Santa Cruz quickly divided the Indios of the surrounding territory among the few dozen Spaniards resident there. But because of the smallpox epidemic of 1589, famine, and flight, the Indian population declined rapidly in the decades following foundation of the city. Father Martínez – the first Jesuit in the region – wrote: "When the Spaniards arrived in that *gobernación* they registered more than 30,000 Indios; when we arrived [1587] there were 10–12,000; and today [1600] I don't believe there are more than 4,000. I refer here to those who have been conquered and pacified, though there are reportedly still many great provinces of infidels."27 In another letter, Martínez asserted that when they arrived "there were 8,000 peaceful Indian tributaries [*de tasa*] who served the Spaniards and more than 1,000 *yanaconas* who worked in their homes and fields."28 But these Indios – the tributaries who were partially obligated to work and the *yanaconas* or servants – were few, while the demand for labor was high: for agricultural work generally, for livestock raising, for the cultivation and weaving of cotton, and for the harvesting and refining of sugar cane. David Block has written: "In this undercapitalized economy, a man's wealth was measured in terms of his control of Indian labor, and, as El Dorado dimmed, interest fell on their labor supply, a trend with long term implications for the savanna peoples."29

We have evidence of at least twenty expeditions into the Llanos during the fifty years after 1590. Many of these went down the Guapay toward its confluence with the Mamoré and in any case followed the rivers into the basin of the upper Madeira. The isolation of the populations there had ended, and periodically contact with the Spaniards took on dramatic tones. Three or four of these expeditions merit mention, both for their size and organizational effort and for their consequences. In 1592, the governor of Santa Cruz, Suárez de Figueroa, received the consent of the viceroy to recruit troops in Charcas under the command of Torres Palomino. In 1595, 150 Spaniards, 300 horses, and a large number of Indian auxiliaries left from Santa Cruz.30 The expedition proceeded slowly, partly by river, and partly over land. In the end, just one detachment continued downriver and made it to the upper Mamoré. They were blocked by the rainy season, lost many horses, suffered from hunger, and had sporadic contact with indigenous populations. They returned to Santa Cruz in 1596, at the end of the rainy season. The Jesuit Jerónimo de Andión was part of the expedition and described its outcome. Writing to the provincial, the Father expressed enthusiasm and zeal for the conversion of the barbarians, but strong doubts about the comportment of the soldiers: "I am certain that the instructions given by the governor [to the captain of the expedition] were just, but I am not sure what happened with regard to their enforcement as the soldiers seemed to pay them no heed."[31] In fact, a few years later, his fellow brother Martínez wrote that "once the rains stopped [. . .], all the soldiers turned back and on the return journey committed the usual atrocities, killing Indios and taking captive any whom they could."[32]

The expedition of Juan de Mendoza Mate de Luna was even more disastrous. Lately arrived from Spain where he had heard about El Dorado from an English gentleman, Mendoza hailed from a powerful family and was appointed governor of Santa Cruz in 1602. He secured ample finances and recruited 130 well-armed soldiers in Potosí, but nonetheless suffered the usual setbacks because of poor preparation, flooding, and hunger. Soldiers accustomed to the high plateau suffered in the tropical clime of the Llanos. Mendoza quickly abandoned the expedition and returned to Santa Cruz, leaving his son in charge of continuing on with about seventy soldiers. Months later, a rescue mission found about ten survivors on the banks of a lagoon and in desperate condition. This poorly organized and disastrous expedition turned the residents of Santa Cruz against the governor, who was subsequently dismissed.

In chapter II, we spoke at length about the voyage of Solís de Holguín in 1617. It was better prepared, included men who were experts on the region, and was smaller in size and well equipped. Contact with the Indios was frequent, and there were battles and the usual capture of men and women. The villages they visited were deserted as the natives by this time viewed the Spanish intruders as a grave threat. But dreams of riches proved to be fantasy and fable. A repeat of the expedition in 1624 (that included the Jesuit Father Navarro) ended with the defection of all its participants.[33] And we have also already seen how the president of the Audiencia de Charcas, Lizarazu, proposed himself to undertake an expedition in 1636–8 but without success.

Finally, the expedition planned by yet another governor of Santa Cruz, Diego de Ampuero, reveals the nature of the relationship between the Spaniards and the Indios of the Llanos. It was described in a letter from the Jesuit Juan de Soto who took part in the expedition, not least because of his knowledge of medicine and surgery.[34] The expedition was authorized by the *cabildo* of Santa Cruz who appointed the captain and other officials, after which "there was a public announcement of the expedition and ninety soldiers, all volunteers and at no cost, were enrolled each signing his name and profession."[35] The goal of the mission was to recapture Indios who had escaped from their masters and from the sugar plantations; though to this was added a request for help from the Mojos tribe of the upper Mamoré against their enemies, the aggressive forest-dwelling Cañacure. The Spaniards took up this request with alacrity as it meant that they would be able to carry out lucrative raids to acquire slaves. They left on 25 August, 1667, with 90 Spaniards, 40 Indian *yanaconas*, and 300 mules. "All were well armed with leather jerkins and shields to protect them from the arrows of the barbarous enemy; all carried guns, swords, and machetes, so they were armed for the attack and to engage in war if the opportunity presented itself."[36] The letter describes an uneventful voyage, arrival among the Mojos, information

received from them, and the subsequent entry into the land
of the Cañacure.

> After having established an encampment in the land of
> the Caña-cure and taken forty or fifty prisoners, don Juan
> Arredondo explored the land and took another ten or
> twelve. He then headed out with forty soldiers and ran into
> a people called the Mazareono, of whom he took seven-
> teen. On his return, Juan Arredondo took another thirty. I
> participated in these raids in order to temper the anger of
> the soldiers, so that it not become excessive, and to care for
> them if they should be wounded, and to inform them of the
> true light and law.[37]

Such were the responsibilities of Juan de Soto, a sort of
physician-chaplain for the expedition. He also made observations regarding strategy: "The frightened Indios hid in the
woods, beaten and cowering in hidden animal lairs, which
pleased the Mojos." And of course he did express a note of
pity:

> It was neither my role nor my mission to challenge the justi-
> fication for these raids and the taking of prisoners. Though
> it was painful to see these Indios lose their freedom and
> be torn away from their lands, parents, siblings, wives, and
> children, to be taken to far away places where they received
> no respite but were treated as slaves in harshest servitude.

Yet de Soto did in fact find a sort of justification:

> For it was shameful that they made war against their friends
> the Mojos, a miserable and unfortunate people who gave
> them no cause for offense nor to be killed and eaten by
> those bestial people. Any prince or king, any lord with a

Table 3.1: Distribution of the Indios seized in the 1667 expedition from Santa Cruz

To Governor Ampuero (absent)	14
Captain Juan Arredondo	14
Sergeant Major Tomas Ribero	8
Vicar D. Pedro Arredondo	5
Captain Domingo Alfonso	5
Captain Franco de Andrade	5
Assistant Hernando de Rivera	5
6 captains and 2 soldiers (4 Indios each)	32
74 soldiers (3 Indios each)	222
Interpreter	1
Total	285

Source: Archivo Nacional de Bolivia, Mojos Complementario, IV, ff. 43–7. In Block, *In Search of El Dorado*, p. 180

sense of humanity would justifiably punish these *Caribe* who seem not to be governed even by natural law. As it turned out, our soldiers came to the aid of their innocent friends who called on them for help because invaded by the Cañacure who attacked them. These latter it was who were dragged into slavery by this expedition which engaged in a just war. As to questions of the legality of these actions, I would not hazard an opinion.[38]

These barbarian Indios, enemies of the friendly Mojos, cannibals (*Caribe*) and so not governed by natural law, could be enslaved according to laws in place from the beginnings of the Conquest.

David Block has found an interesting document that lists the prey captured and their distribution, fairly equal, between the participants of the expedition (see table 3.1). The consequences of and reactions to expeditions of this sort for Indios who were not friendly with the Spaniards are easy to imagine. The frontier residents of Santa Cruz did not behave much differently from the Portuguese *bandeirantes* carrying out their *malocas* (slaving raids); following presumably approved procedures, though, their expeditions enjoyed a veneer of legality.

In the letter/reports already referred to, Father Martínez offered convincing examples of the good reasons the Indios had for avoiding the Spaniards:

> The region of the Xarais lies on the banks of the Paraguay about seventy leagues from the city of Santa Cruz; large and well populated it was relatively well controlled and obedient. Then in 1599–1600 an armed band of Spaniards went there and without cause or reason for complaint, the captains inflicted great harm and damage to the Indios, killing many and taking prisoner all they could, depriving them of their property, their food, their children, and their wives. Most fled into the woods and so, because of the atrocities and destruction of the soldiers, the opportunity for conversion was lost.[39]

And again:

> The province of the Paretis was discovered at the end of 1599; it lies about 100 leagues north of Santa Cruz. The Spaniards discovered eleven villages there, and the soldiers committed a quantity of barbarous acts. It happened that 200 Indios came to them in peace and were closed in a large house where they were held for three or four days without food. When out of extreme necessity the Indios tried to leave the house, they were met with shots from harquebuses and sword blades; most were taken as slaves to Santa Cruz.[40]

More than a century later the demand for slaves and servants in Santa Cruz had not been satisfied. To that end, the residents there took advantage of their exclusive right to organize expeditions among the infidels of the Llanos. Indeed they convinced their governor, José Cayetano Hurtado de Ávila, to organize an expedition against the Itonamas who bordered on peaceful and converted Indios 200 leagues from Santa Cruz. That undertaking violated the repeated decrees from the Audiencia de Charcas that forbade these sorts of enterprises. It included massacres and the taking of prisoners practically under the eyes of Father Garriga, a Jesuit superior visiting the nearby missions, and led not only to a condemnation but to a royal ordinance that read as follows:

> In spite of the fact that the residents of the Indies know well the laws and ordinances and that expeditions of this sort are contrary to Royal directives, the named don José Cayetano and the residents of Santa Cruz de la Sierra, without any cause or motive other than self-interest, entered into the land of the Ytonamas, more than 200 leagues from Santa Cruz, crossing pacified regions in part converted by the missionaries of the Company, as this land of the Ytonamas borders on the Reductions of San Pedro, San Joaquín, La Concepción, and San Julián, and they were already on friendly terms with the missionaries; the aforementioned governor and residents carried out all manner of atrocity and violence: burning, killing, and taking captive as many as 2000 people, children and adults, imprisoning them and conducting them with great hardship to the city of Santa Cruz.[41]

The ordinance instructed that the slaves be freed, and the guilty punished, depriving them of their offices and expelling them from the region.

There are various bits and pieces of evidence, referring to frequent actions undertaken by individuals or small groups

whose inspiration cannot have been much different from
that of the large, organized, and well-financed expeditions.
When the Jesuits resolved a few years later to extend their
work of conversion to the Llanos, they encountered a land
sewn with resentment and suspicion. Though rarely aggressive, the Indios were reluctant to establish contact and quick
to retreat and disappear. The Fathers had to win them over
slowly and with great patience.

IV

THE ROUND-UP OF INDIAN SLAVES COMES
TO AN END WHILE THE CONTEST FOR THEIR
SOULS BEGINS. A CHAPLAIN-PHYSICIAN
AND A POLYGLOT MISSIONARY. HATCHETS,
WEDGES, AND KNIVES IN EXCHANGE FOR
OBEDIENCE. CATHEDRAL OF MUD AND WOOD
WITH THREE NAVES

By the last decades of the seventeenth century the myth of El
Dorado had faded, while the nature of the Llanos Indios was
better and better understood. Santa Cruz de la Sierra was
an important outpost for the Viceroyalty and in a position
to control access to Alto Perú and Potosí from the Rio de la
Plata region. It was a conduit that the Portuguese of Brazil
would have happily seized in order to intercept the goods
and riches that flowed along it. The broad spaces around
Santa Cruz were well suited to livestock and to plantation
crops like cotton and sugar cane. Though the Llanos were
hundreds of kilometers away, the Santa Cruz residents considered the populations there to be a potential and important

source of labor. Certainly the few religious who accompanied the exploratory and raiding expeditions – including the Jesuits Andión in 1595, Villarnao in 1617, Navarro in 1624, and de Soto in 1667 – were unlikely to either moderate the appetite of the colonists or succeed in saving the souls of the barbarians. Nor, as we have seen, did ordinances and protests from the Audiencia de Charcas, the viceroy of Perú, or the court against slaving raids have much impact beyond the Andes.

At this same time the Jesuit evangelical campaign was enjoying its greatest successes: the network of missions in Paraguay had been established and the spiritual, social, and economic governance of the Guaraní fully developed. And the Company of Jesus had established flourishing missions in other places as well: in 1637 the Sardinian Jesuit Father Cugia and a companion had worked their way down the Marañón, passing through the dangerous rapids at Pongo de Manseriche, and founded the first Amazon mission. Fifteen years later there were already thirteen missions on the banks of the Marañón, Ucayali, and Huallaga rivers, covering an extension of more than 1,000 kilometers.[1] Farther to the north, between 1625 and 1653, the Llanos of the Orinoco network of missions was established between the Meta and Casanare rivers, later simply called the "Orinoco Missions" (see map 7).[2]

The Jesuits arrived in Perú in 1568, later than the other missionary religious orders; the Augustinians, the Dominicans, the Franciscans, and the Mercedarians had all preceded them. The number of religious regulars there at the end of the sixteenth century already exceeded 1,500. "In the first third of the seventeenth century, the gospel arrived in all those parts of the kingdom inhabited by indigenous peoples of a certain level of culture and who had been incorporated into the Incan state."[3] Nonetheless, given the

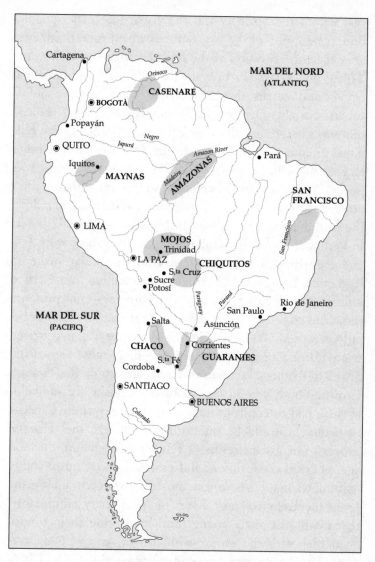

7 *The missions of South America*

vast size of the territory and the dispersion of the population, penetration of the true faith remained superficial, even
after the concentration of the Indios carried out by Viceroy
Toledo in 1670–80: a thin shell covering a base of ancient
beliefs and rituals that re-emerged whenever the political and social control of the Spaniards was relaxed. Toledo
moreover had to use all of his influence to convince the religious to come out of their convents in Lima and the other
large centers in order to undertake missionary work. It is
said that he was himself persuaded to take the initiative after
attending a service in the Lima cathedral that was overflowing with these same religious. In 1595 there were 242 Jesuits
in Perú, between priests and monks; in 1615 there were 370,
and even though the large territories that today make up
Argentina, Paraguay, and Uruguay were shifted from Perú to
a new "Province of Paraguay," the Peruvian Jesuit presence
remained 400–500 for the rest of the century and regularly exceeded 500 in the eighteenth century.[4] They arrived
from Europe in groups of ten to thirty; most were from
Spain but others came from lands subject to the Spanish
Crown. Youth was an important prerequisite for individuals who had to confront long journeys and primitive modes
of living. It would be interesting to analyze the selection
process, not just in terms of religious conviction, but also
age, physical constitution, and practical or technical ability
and knowledge.[5] There was moreover concern among the
Jesuit hierarchy to resist a sort of "missionary enthusiasm"
that infatuated many young brothers, urging them toward
encounter with the exotic, with danger, and with martyr-
dom. The Neapolitan Geronimo Pallas, who reached Perú
at the beginning of the seventeenth century, wrote a long
manual based on his own experience and focusing among
other things on the need to distinguish genuine motivations
from false ones. The false ones included the desire to see

new lands, to improve one's situation, to support distant parents, and above all "the desire to live among proud and barbarous peoples, to suffer hardships and risk death, to be the first to bring the gospel to new lands, to convert and baptize many heathen souls, and to wear the crown of the martyr."[6] According to the rational Father, these last motivations were positive for a missionary but also dangerous because "they may hide vanity and the desire to accomplish these things not for good in and of itself, but for the honor and fame that go with them."[7]

The Jesuits arrived in Santa Cruz de la Sierra in 1587 and throughout the seventeenth century never numbered more than ten. Together with a few Mercedarians and a few clerics, they had the task, not an easy one, of preaching to the coarse colonists and indoctrinating the Indios who lived and worked in the Spanish homes, farms, and missions. They were also to carry out evangelical work among the Indian tributaries, who lived spread out in a range of 50 to 100 kilometers, and among more distant and difficult ethnicities, like the indomitable Chiriguanos.[8]

In the Llanos, hundreds of kilometers from Santa Cruz, the Jesuits had accompanied various expeditions but had never attempted missionary work. Their first tentative effort, which ended in failure, started out on 10 September, 1668, one year after the expedition and raid that yielded 285 Indian captives (see chapter III). The Jesuit expedition was also a military one and included 80 soldiers, 30 *yanaconas*, 500 Indian auxiliaries, and 330 mules. Fathers José Bermudo and Juan de Soto, whom we have already met as participants in the expedition of the previous year, took part and reported to the provincial.[9] The expedition made it to the upper Mamoré among the friendly Mojos; there in a "well-formed" village on the bank of the river and donated to them by a *cacique*, the Jesuits founded the short-lived Mission of the Holy Trinity.

Bermudo stopped there, but de Soto continued on with the expedition as its chaplain-physician. They made it to the land of a rival tribe whom de Soto called "Estolicanos" (they used dart-throwing rods, or *estolicas*, as weapons):

> Fiercely proud *caribe* (cannibals) who feed on human flesh when they can find it, men and women both go about naked; they live on the barren pampas where there is neither bush nor stream; they drink water from the lagoons and stagnant puddles and work their fields intensively with great order and care; they eat only yucca and maize and are fearsome to look at.

Nonetheless, they were defeated by the Spaniards who "took 240 *piezas* (persons), a multitude of baby girls and boys and women; the Spaniards divided them up, two *piezas* each" (though apparently many more for the leaders or the numbers don't work out).[10] The potential conquest was large: thirty-three or forty villages – eighty according to some – of up to 200 inhabitants each. Bermudo referred to eighty villages that stretched over 70 leagues for a total of 4,800 souls. He had found the Mojos to be of good "disposition" and believed their conversion was possible. What was needed then to begin missionary work was the arrival of other Fathers, beasts of burden, and goods for trade (especially needles, knives, hooks, wedges, glass pearls, etc.). Given that the best steel products came from Lima, it was necessary to obtain them there, send them to Chuquisaca and then Santa Cruz, and then by canoe to the village. De Soto's proposal represents an entirely new sort of evangelical program for the region, one that contrasted starkly with the accompanying military expedition and raid, even if among an enemy tribe. It became clear, however, to the Fathers themselves and especially to their superiors, that missionary work had to be clearly separated from the interests of the colonists. This first military-missionary expedition had instead an interesting appendix: in late July of the following year (1669), Juan de Soto returned to Santa Cruz "with ten canoes and many Indios including the principal *caciques* of the villages near to ours [the settlement of Bermudo and de Soto] [. . .]. The latter carried out their exchanges with the pieces of cloth they brought with them."[11] The narrator is Father Julian de Áller who set off with de Soto, stayed among the Mojos for less than a month, and wrote a highly optimistic report to his provincial. They had turned down the offer of a military escort from the governor, a choice made "because [. . .] word had gotten round that our intention was to deceive and pacify the people so that, once they felt reassured, the Spaniards could 'enter' and take control of them."[12] Father Áller describes the Indios as mild and courteous, well disposed to becoming Christians, not idolatrous, and lacking in political structure as the *caciques* only took command in case of war. He also offers information about their lifestyle, food, clothing, occupations, agriculture, and so on. Conversion activity was limited as they only proffered baptism *in articulo mortis*. Áller's greatest contribution – he knew Guaraní well – was linguistic. During his short stay he compiled a rudimentary grammar-vocabulary. Among other things, he noted a certain frequency of Spanish words, evidence of contact with the surrounding Hispanic world and with the Spaniards themselves.[13]

The activities of Bermudo and de Soto did not continue much after the return of Áller (de Soto died in Santa Cruz in 1672). They may have been hampered by the opposition of a few members of their host village, fearful that the Fathers were going to open up the way for the Spaniards of Santa Cruz.[14] An effective missionary program required a number of things – authorization from the superiors of the

Order, logistical organization, more or less stable contact, and money – and although requested, the needed support was not forthcoming. Just the same, the Llanos were no longer a region of mystery. The access routes and geography were well known, as were the characteristics of many of the ethnicities residing there, the types of settlement, anthropological and social characteristics, and the approximate size of the population. These were all essential elements for an effective missionary program, one that as the leadership of the Company well knew would have to be sharply separated from any sort of military activity.

Five years later, in 1674, the climate for a serious attempt at establishing missions in the Llanos had improved, though several more years of effort were needed before inauguration of the first Mission-Reduction of Loreto in 1682, after which others followed in quick succession. The vice provincial, Father Hernando Cavero, authorized the establishment of a mission in the land of the Mojos with a letter of precise instructions written to Father Marbán, who was nominated superior of the mission, Father Cipriano Barace, and their confrere José del Castillo; the latter two had only recently arrived from Perú. Marbán was twenty-seven years old and Barace thirty-three.[15] Mindful that the previous missions had failed for various reasons, Cavero described the new attempt as an experiment and instructed that "the primary goal of this mission will be exploratory, so that using the things that they see and that they learn we can make the correct decision." Cavero then went on to more precise instructions regarding the need to gather information about:

- the layout of the villages, their number, and the people who reside in each one throughout the province;
- how well disposed the people are to receive the doctrine of the Holy Gospel, with what attitude they will receive

it, and if they respond to the arrival of Marbán and his
company with happiness or repugnance;

- whether the nation of the Mojos speaks one language
  or many; so that it can more easily be learned, you will
  take along the glossary put together by P. Julian de Áller
  which can be found in Santa Cruz;
- whether there are other nations nearby; what are they
  called and how large are their populations;
- how many days march it is from the *embarcadero* to the
  zone of residence;
- whether the place where they will choose to establish
  their main residence is appropriate, whether the climate
  is healthy, what are the environmental conditions of the
  mission and what sorts of sustenance are available, including for the survival of our own;
- the customs, rites, and ceremonies of the barbarians;
  their vices, virtues, and inclinations in their natural state;
  whether there is great danger for the lives of our own
  among these Indios and if the missionaries can with
  some security carry out the work of conversion; for this
  purpose it is important that at the beginning the three
  brothers stay together, never separating for more than a
  few days, and organizing their chapel and home in such
  a way that no Indian women or girls enter into them, so
  that they understand that the home of our own is closed
  to any sort of female;
- what hope there is in the future for the establishment
  by the Company of this mission; and if the prospects
  look good, how many objects will need to be brought as
  gifts.[16]

The three were given a year to gather the required information and visit the region. They were absolutely forbidden
to take with them any sort of military escort. Just as they were

also forbidden to take any *piezas* (slaves), a ban that extended also to the two interpreters who accompanied them. At the end of the year, they were to draft and sign a report, including explanation of dissenting opinions. The expedition was financed with 500 pesos that had been left by a resident of Potosí for the conversion of the infidels. With that money they would be able to acquire at Chuquisaca the necessary *rescates* (tools, tin, trinkets) for trade and payments.

In compiling his list of instructions, Father Cavero clearly had previous experiences in the Llanos in mind, experiences that had been for the most part unfortunate. As it turned out, the expedition did not get underway until a year later (28 June, 1675). In the meantime, del Castillo had gone ahead alone in search of canoes and auxiliaries. He made his way back up the Guapay a few months later and arrived in Santa Cruz with fifteen boats and sixty Indios, confirmation that the Mojos would welcome the expedition. As instructed, the three missionaries completed their report to Father Cavero one year later (it is dated 20 April, 1676).[17] It is a wordy and often evasive text that repeats much that was already known. The Fathers were only able to visit a small part of the region and offer as justification the fact that they contracted malaria and that the rainy season interrupted their activities. The report includes little in the way of direct observation and is based largely on hearsay and information supplied by the Mojos themselves: there are about eighty villages containing some 6,000 souls; the Indios are well disposed to conversion but their motivation is ambiguous and in any case the Fathers' experience was limited to the one village in which they lived; the missionaries will not have to worry for their lives (in spite of the report of an Augustinian who was murdered and stripped of the silver he was carrying while coming down the mountain from Cochabamba); after the departure of Áller, the Mojos suffered incursions from free *mulattos* and *mestizos* coming from Santa Cruz who carried out slaving raids; there is evidence of regular contact and trade with the Spaniards of Santa Cruz, with textiles exchanged for utensils and trinkets. The Fathers completed their report with the observation that their evangelical work should continue and the request for four more missionaries. Judging from his later pronouncements, chances are that Father Barace was unhappy with this report. A few years later he expressed his own dissent in another letter. According to Barace, the population did not number more than 3,600 and the villages were small. He thought that carrying out an operation like that in Paraguay where the reductions might number over 5,000 souls was impossible; at best they might achieve 400 among the Mojos. Nor was he convinced regarding the inclinations and motivations of the Mojos to conversion – he thought them ambiguous and practical – or the attitude of his colleagues who based their optimistic hopes for the future on vague conjecture.[18]

Neither it seems was Father Cavero overly impressed with the report of the three missionaries, judging from a sort of "ordinance" that he issued after consulting with the other Fathers of the province (8 December, 1676).[19] He felt that the situation called for more careful consideration and more time. To that end he nominated another mission to be headed by the Jesuit superior of Santa Cruz, Father Martin Lituria, and including another Father and another confrère. This group was to meet up with the other three missionaries and, once they had adjusted to the situation, create a second residence, whence they could specify which territories and villages would depend upon which residence and so begin the general work of contact and exploration. This work was meant to be undertaken with both the peoples living along the Mamoré and its tributaries and also those on the adjacent pampas. They were to determine the name of the ethnicity in each village as well as their locations and population sizes and the distances between the villages.

This work took months but paid off, as revealed in the report that Fathers Marbán, Ygarza, and Barace presented to Father Luis Sotelo whom the provincial had sent to gauge the progress of the enterprise. Based on four months of investigation, the report (see chapter II) offered a point-by-point response to the ordinance of late 1676. Sotelo himself had been given instructions to end the experiment if he found the situation unsatisfactory – there were rumors about difficulties encountered by the missionary Fathers. The *caciques* had been issued a sort of ultimatum – "they were threatened" – and

> having received benefits and gifts, they had come to look well upon the Fathers and, fearing to lose those benefits, they offered to obey the Fathers in whatever they commanded. They quickly took up the sacred doctrine and derived much benefit from it. They did not object when the Fathers beat their children if they were lazy [in learning the sacred doctrine]; indeed they themselves were the first to criticize the children and showed humility regarding the corporal punishment [*corrección de mano*] the Fathers inflicted on them for their shortcomings.[20]

The visiting Father declared himself satisfied and allowed the mission to continue with reinforcements – several of the Fathers had fallen ill and returned to Santa Cruz. The principal aim was to convince the *caciques* and Indios to form larger settlements as this was the key to success in any missionary effort among dispersed populations. Indeed without the creation of reductions, any attempt to indoctrinate and control, to impose discipline and order, was vain. The *operarios* (religious) were brought from Europe at too great a cost and with too much effort to be employed in risky and unproductive projects. Yet the work of reduction and concentration was hard and faced numerous obstacles: the fear that larger concentrations would encourage slave raiders; the loss of mobility that was an important strategy for coping with the natural conditions of the Llanos; the reluctance of Indios speaking different languages or dialects to live together; and finally the difficulty of choosing suitable locations for the settlements. Father Barace – probably the most insightful and critical of the missionaries – offered a vivid picture of the difficulties overcome and those still in the future:

> Already among the Indios in this province we are encountering less resistance than before when it comes to gathering them together in each *parcialidad* of the territory, because when the visiting Father arrived there was great fear that we would abandon them, that they would lose the advantages they have gained, and that the Spaniards would move against them. But they recognize that we offer some protection and with time have calmed down with the realization that we are not gathering them together in order to take them away as prisoners; and so their fear has decreased though they remain cautious. But what attracts them most are the many goods they receive when we pay them for dwellings or purchase canoes; or when we provide them with the tools needed to build houses or canoes or to farm the fields. In this way and with these human resources we have created four villages. The first is made up of the Aracureonos and lies high up the river; it has about 360 souls, young and old, and counting those who still need to arrive should come to number 380. The inhabitants of this *parcialidad* wanted to throw me in the river, as I will describe below. Many men in this village have two wives, but I have learned from the Indios that they separated on learning that they would

have to give them up. But I don't know if they really did. Going down the river a distance equivalent to ten days of return travel, we chose a site last year for the Suberionos. But they did not want to go there and would not budge. Continuing downstream one comes upon the village of the Casaboyonos, that has 160 inhabitants, and then further down our own which is in a wooded area and has at least 400. These three villages all speak the same language. Further down there is another village of 280 natives that speak another language. [. . .] These villages will have to be left in this arrangement and at about these sizes, first of all because the sites are of limited extent and secondly because it is unclear where we might find other inhabitants; optimistically our own village may reach 500. [. . .] It is clear to me that the real reason for the success of the transfer of natives is not our faith, but their own self-interest: give me a knife, a machete, a splitting wedge, or a plate and there you have the real reason for which they come to live in our villages; and no-one adds "I come so that you can baptize me and teach me the Christian doctrine and the law of God."[21]

In 1682 the long work of preparation led to the formal initiation of the missionary system of the Mojos with the founding, on the Feast of the Annunciation, of the Nuestra Señora de Loreto Mission. This mission, however, comprised a series of separate villages, an inconvenience that led to their being further grouped together. Father Orellana, who took part in the foundation of Loreto, described it this way:

On that day [of the foundation] more than 500 souls were baptized and subsequently all the rest who were in the village and numbered over 600. Christian customs began to spread among them and every day became better rooted.

The next year three other villages with 650 souls that belong to this reduction [of Loreto] were baptized. After that, many others were baptized in addition to the babies, children of the Indios already mentioned, so that today [1687] there are more than 2,000 Christians and there would be many more if continuous relocations did not slow us down. It is usual for the Indios to relocate their villages for various reasons, the principal one being the changeability of the river that either divides the villages or gets too close to them, because in less than six years the river has altered its course four times and it is changing again now. During these relocations it is impossible to indoctrinate the Indios. For this reason we are considering whether it would not be better if all the natives belonging to the reduction resided in just one village, which would have to be ours.

There were numerous difficulties involved in choosing a new site, but after a great deal of cajoling the Indios of Loreto were gathered together in a single village: "there are 2,300 people in all, though they speak three distinct languages, and that is one of the greatest obstacles to their rapid conversion. So as part of the process of concentrating all of them in one village we hope also to get them to adopt a single language and have already begun that effort."[22] Orellana also reports that another reduction, among the Mayumanes, had been started the previous year (1686); it lay 12 leagues from Loreto and was called La Santísima Trinidad (today the most important city in the Beni Department):

There is already a rapidly growing village of many people who are being gathered together and converted, though it requires a great deal of work as there is not much straw for their houses, but the desire to congregate is great and motivates them to search far and wide. At the beginning of next

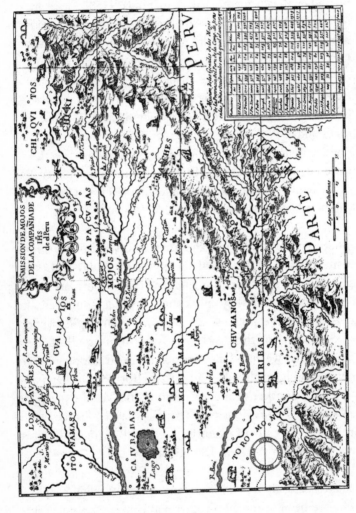

8 Eighteenth-century map of the Llanos (the box on the right includes the planilla for 1713)

year they should number more than 2,000 souls of whom we will be able to baptize 1,000; the others will take more time as they speak other languages.[23]

The work then of persuasion, reduction, and conversion had begun, though, as these accounts attest, it was not a simple process. The Fathers had to learn the lay of the land; get to know the various regions and peoples; show themselves to have come as friends by means of actions and exchanges that benefited the Indios; allay the suspicions, resentment, and hostility inspired by the conquering Spanish; and learn both the language and the essential psychology of the indigenous cultures. Then came the difficult work of gathering together and "reducing" at a single place people that were spread among small villages of a few dozen inhabitants and far apart from one another. It was a task that required tipping the balance of costs and benefits in the Indios' favor. Principal among the benefits were material ones: a splitting wedge or a steel ax reduced the work time needed to cut down a tree, build a house, or make a canoe – today we would say increased productivity – by an order of magnitude or more. Similarly, the protection that the Fathers could offer, both from enemy tribes and especially from marauding Spaniards, weighed heavily among the benefits. The costs instead included contact with ethnicities from whom one had lived apart, the confusion of languages and cultures, reduced mobility, and the loss of autonomy in the choice of where to live. Once the balance tipped in the right direction the project could begin. Such were the necessary and unavoidable material and social bases for any attempt to control and influence the Indios and so to begin the projects of conversion and baptism, the indoctrination of children, and the elimination of "barbaric" customs like collective ceremonial drunkenness, polygamy, and the killing of newborns in cases where the mother dies in childbirth. The missionary experience among the Mojos, described here in the words of the protagonists themselves, bears many similarities to the parallel experiences of Jesuits in other parts of the continent.

After its foundation in 1682 and subsequent relocation downriver from the confluence of the Guapay and Mamoré, Loreto became in 1684 the command post of the missionary project.[24] The second mission was La Santísima Trinidad de los Mayumanes (founded in 1686 by Father Barace), 12 leagues downstream from Loreto, followed by San Ignacio de los Punuanas (founded in 1689 by Orellana), 14 leagues west of Trinidad near the vast territories of the Cañacure (the same who suffered slaving raids in 1667 and 1668, events described in sad tones by Father Bermudo). Next came San Francisco Javier (founded in 1689 by the tireless Barace), 8 leagues down from Trinidad; then San José de los Mabarenos (founded in 1691 by Father Espejo) at the foot of the Cordillera opposite the valley of Cochabamba; and San Francisco de Borja de los Churimanas, 12 leagues from San José (1693, again by Espejo). Over the course of eleven years, six missions had been founded comprising a population of nearly 20,000 Indios. Three of these were on or near the Mamoré along a north–south axis (Loreto, Trinidad, and San Javier, to which San Pedro was added in 1697). Three others (San Ignacio, San José – to which the nearby San Luis Gonzaga was added in 1698 – and San Borja) lay on an east–west line in the western pampas that led right up to the base of the Andes. Based on information supplied by his subordinates, Provincial Father Diego de Eguiluz compiled his *Historia de la Misión de Mojos*[25] in 1696. In it he relates that between 1682 and 1695 in the six missions: "a total of 19,759 people were pacified and brought to lead a Christian life [. . .] of these we baptized 10,319 souls, bringing them the sacraments of the Church and the virtues of primitive

Christianity, not to mention the countless little angels who thanks to baptism sailed happily to heaven."[26] He adds, though, that this was all accomplished at the cost of:

> much sweat, effort, and difficulty, walking for one or two solid months, through swamps and up to the knees in mud, under a burning sun, beset by insects and mosquitoes, surviving on maize and bananas, sleeping on sand banks stretched out on the ground or in the forest equipped with a hammock, among barbarian Indios and cannibals, learning new languages every day; yet happy and content to be guiding an ever larger group of heathens and not a band of soldiers intent on wealthy booty; their tunics filthy, their feet wounded, their face and hands torn at by the dense wood.[27]

Half of the 20,000 Indios were baptized, and in 1695 the missions were run by twenty-three religious (nineteen priests and four brothers).[28] Loreto had a large central plaza with a church with three naves, 50 meters long and 16 meters wide, entirely built of *adobe* because of the lack of stone; it was well decorated and its three altars were adorned with cedar *retablos* painted by children under the direction of one of the Fathers. The home of the religious with a cloister and the public buildings were situated on the central plaza. Around the plaza the village had large roads laid out in a gridwork according to the much-used colonial model.[29] Similar structures were built for the other missions, and only San Francisco de Borja, the last to be founded, still used a large hut for its church. San Ignacio, run by Father Orellana, had a church still grander than that of Loreto and was made up of three *parcialidades*, each with a different language, though the intention was that Mojo come to predominate. Orellana tried to find a path over the Andes that would drive straight to Cochabamba – the closest Spanish city as the crow flies on the Peruvian plateau – and so avoid the long detour via Santa Cruz; del Castillo had disappeared making a similar attempt in 1688.[30] In the vast region that reached from the Mamoré to the foot of the Andes, the six villages were far from one another; the closest neighbor was 40 to 80 kilometers away, a distance that could be covered in one or two days by canoe when the conditions were favorable. The Fathers alternated making regular visits to the immense hinterland in hopes of attracting new converts to their villages and to lay groundwork for the founding of additional missions. On one of these voyages Father Barace entered into the land of the Baures; twenty years later the attempt to convert them would cost him his life. The enterprising Jesuit also succeeded in driving a herd of cattle from Santa Cruz to Loreto: although the herd numbered hundreds on departure only eighty-six arrived at destination, more than enough in any case to begin a flourishing cattle-raising enterprise.[31]

Jesuit expansion slowed at the end of the seventeenth century as the result of a rebellion against a Dominican mission situated at the foot of the Andes which spread to San Borja in 1696–7 and required intervention from Santa Cruz.[32] It started up again with the conversion of the Movima on the western pampas (the missions of Santísimos Reyes in 1702 and Santa Rosa in 1705) and then expansion among the Baures. In 1700, Father Altamirano, provincial at the time and a man of strong will, visited four of the missions among the Mojos. He was the first provincial to visit Santa Cruz – viewed from Perú as a desolate outpost– not to mention the Llanos. At the end of his visit he gathered together the Fathers at Loreto to discuss the current situation of the missions and how to proceed in the future.[33] It is Altamirano himself who informs us regarding the principal initiatives of the missionary project. The first was language: many different languages were spoken and it was important to impose Mojo as the *lingua franca*. It was decided to publish at Lima a Mojo grammar and catechism prepared by Father Marbán which would serve as a text for teaching children so that the new generations would learn both the Mojo language and Catholic doctrine. The second was self-government. The Jesuits resolved to elect every year in each reduction two *alcaldes*, four *regidores*, one *ejecutor*, one *procurador*, and one *portero*; together they would consititute the *cabildo*, all of course under the supreme command of the Fathers. In this the Llanos Jesuits followed the example of their brethren in Paraguay; a simulacrum of civil government served not only the purpose of management and control, but also assigned roles of importance to those, like the *caciques*, who had lost some of their traditional influence. Third, the Jesuits wanted to encourage agricultural development. Although the Mojos had always managed to feed themselves, the reductions presumably created the difficulty of finding sufficient cultivable land near the villages and protected from flooding. Moreover, it was hoped to reduce dependence on hunting, an activity that required too free a lifestyle and frequent absences from the villages, a degree of autonomy incompatible with the order imposed by the Jesuits. Plans included the introduction of new crops (wheat did not thrive, but the cassava of Paraguay, with which could be made a sort of bread, yielded good results as did rice), instruction in the use of ox and plough, and the creation of communal fields for the cultivation of sugar cane, cotton, and legumes. Altamirano was also pleased to note the spread among the Indios of handicrafts:

Either directly themselves or by means of skilled brother assistants, the missionaries instruct the Indios in handicrafts of which they were ignorant and which are necessary for civil and religious life: carpentry, masonry, blacksmithing, tailoring, shoemaking and the like. They have also taught rudimentary care of wounds and illness, and for this brothers versed in medicine and surgery have come and they are very useful, no less so than any other missionary.[34]

In the first years of the eighteenth century, missionary action turned to the region of the Baures. Considered by the Jesuits to be a more developed tribe than the Mojos, the Baures lived in the wooded north-eastern part of the Llanos among the intricacies of the upper Iténez and Guaporé rivers. In the brief time between 1709 and 1720 six missions were founded: Concepción, San Joaquín, San Juan Bautista, San Martín, San Nicolas, and Santa María Magdalena. Three more were added between 1725 and 1744: San Miguel, Patrocinio Beata Virgen María, and San Simón. Already by 1720, however, the Llanos network of missions had reached maturity with a population of 35,000 Indios, close to the maximum reached during the entire period of Jesuit control (see map 9).

The conversion of the Baures started badly. Father Barace, who directed the Trinidad mission, had traveled there frequently and established good contacts with an eye to founding new reductions among the Baures. In 1702 at the end of the rainy season he undertook another voyage accompanied by four Mojos and a mule carrying the usual gifts and a portable altar. He passed through villages that he had visited before and then entered into unknown territory. There, in one village, he met with open hostility and was pursued, attacked, and killed. The Mojos traveling with him managed to escape and return to Trinidad.[35] Father Altamirano furnishes a softened account of the events that followed:

It then happened that the governor of Santa Cruz [. . .] don Benito de la Rivera y Quiroga sent as punishment for that offense 1,000 armed Christian Indios and a good number

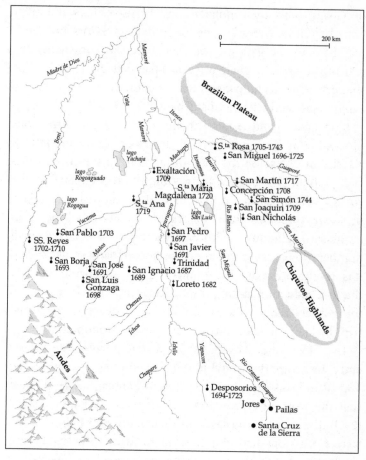

9 Missions of the Llanos de Mojos with the dates of foundation

of Spanish soldiers, directed less by military discipline and more by the instructions of the missionaries that they not inflict too great a punishment and so inspire hatred among the infidels for the True Faith.[36]

The expedition was also meant to survey the region, take note of its expanse and natural habitat, and the number of villages and their populations. "The soldiers did their Christian duty. Arresting the identified aggressors and sending them to the gallows, they succeeded in convincing the rest of the error of their ways and pacified the land."[37] The soldiers who accompanied the missionaries were able to explore the land without disturbance.

Conversion and establishment of the Baures missions proceeded at the rapid rhythm described above in spite of a series of obstacles: the long distance from the Mojos missions (about 50 leagues from Loreto); the danger of the voyage which passed through land of hostile tribes; the lack of *rescates* (precious goods for trade); and above all the small number of religious – "although there were 34, such a small number of harvesters could not gather so many souls."[38] And it is worth noting that the foundation of Concepción (in 1709 the first reduction among the Baures) was far from easy, and the Fathers required a cavalry escort in order to make the trip through the lands of the inhospitable Itonomas.[39]

In 1713 Father Messia reported that thirty-seven priests and four brothers worked in the sixteen missions and served 30,512 Indios who spoke twenty-four languages. He claimed that the work of conversion had achieved excellent results; the Indios were enthusiastic in their faith, and fifteen of the sixteen missions had churches, many with three naves and richly adorned by the Indios who were excellent carvers and painters. All of the holy days were celebrated with great gatherings of the people, processions, decorations, lights, and singing. Meanwhile, the Fathers maintained an iron grip:

They established the following [rules] in order to suppress violations and so that punishments meted out would serve as a warning to others and all would live with caution and fear. At the beginning of the year the *alcaldes, regidores, procuradores,* and *fiscales* are selected. They carry signs of their office which mark them off from the rest and have places reserved for them in church. They are collectively responsible for maintaining order in the village, encouraging good habits, investigating violations, and punishing the guilty. They attend seriously to their tasks, making the rounds and maintaining a vigil over the village day and night so that all fear them and so refrain from bad behavior and do not deviate from the law of God that most observe.[40]

At the peak of missionary work between 1720 and 1750, the Llanos was covered by a network of over twenty missions governed by about fifty religious and comprising 30–40,000 Indios. Their distribution had been radically altered by the Jesuits' projects of reduction-aggregation, while their linguistic, ethnic, and cultural complexity had been simplified. As compared to Paraguay – where in 1730 the thirty Jesuit missions counted more than 140,000 inhabitants – the Llanos reductions were more spread out and smaller (in 1730 they averaged 1,600 inhabitants as compared to about 5,000 in Paraguay).[41] Unfortunately, as we explore below, the statistical sources for the Llanos are far less eloquent than those of Paraguay, and this fact limits our ability to understand the demographic and social circumstances of the Mojos. Figure A.1 reports the progress of the population in the mission system – and then under civil administration following expulsion of the Jesuits in 1767 – from 1691 to 1888. The first part of the graph, till about 1720, shows the upward curve associated with the missionary project; it then declines after 1750 as a result of a combination of negative demographic and political developments. The late nineteenth-century drop is the result above all of emigration linked to the rubber boom in the Amazon forest. As we shall see, it is impossible to separate out the demo-anthropological behavior of the Mojos from the influence of external factors. During the demographic peak – 1720–50 – the natural/administrative districts of the Mamoré and of the Baures (so defined after the departure of the Jesuits) were the largest and about the same size, while the third district, the Pampas, declined in relative importance.

V

THE GOOD FATHERS CONFRONT THE LOOSE
HABITS OF THE MOJOS. A STRAW MAT,
TWO GEESE, AND TWO SPINDLES MAKE
UP THE BRIDE'S DOWRY. THE INDIOS AND
DISEASE: STOIC OR HEALTHY? PORTUGUESE
AND SPANIARDS AT WAR ON THE EDGE OF
THE SWAMP. THE SAD EXPULSION OF THE
FATHERS IN 1768: TWENTY-FOUR LEAVE BUT
ONLY FOURTEEN ARRIVE.

The history of the American Indios after 1492 is bitter and complex, and there is much still to learn. The size of the indigenous population at the moment of contact with Europeans is nearly "unknowable." It has inspired heated disputes that find on one side those who believe the continent was well populated (in some areas reaching densities greater than those of the more developed European societies of the day) and others who maintain that the Americas were a primitive land with few inhabitants surviving on subsistence agriculture and hunting and gathering, save in the Aztec and

Incan empires. These different positions have led to population estimates for the continent around 1500 ranging from 8 to 113 million.[1] There is instead general consensus that following contact the indigenous population embarked upon a downward trajectory that has been variously described as a catastrophe, a crisis, or a serious decline. Evaluations of the population made by the Spanish administration in the second half of the sixteenth century leave little doubt in this regard. The scale of that decline in relation to the unknown initial population cannot be determined, but whether it declined by a third, by half, or by 90 percent (as many maintain), it certainly suffered a violent demographic shock from which it recovered only gradually in the centuries that followed. Scientific debate in recent decades has focused on the causes of this decline. Temporary victor in this debate has been the epidemiological hypothesis which links the crisis to new viral diseases (measles and smallpox) imported from Europe and their devastating impact on the indigenous populations, as those populations lacked the immunities that Old World populations had developed over the centuries or millennia of coexistence with these diseases. Comparative reflection, however, of the American situation and the variability of different histories – from the disappearance of entire populations (the Taíno of the Caribbean) at one extreme to the consolidation of others (the Guaraní of Paraguay) at the opposite one – urge a re-evaluation of the direct testimonies coming from the first phase of the Conquest. Those witnesses, whether named Las Casas or Oviedo, whether governors or religious, *encomenderos* or men of arms, were convinced that the demographic crisis playing out dramatically before their eyes was not simply caused by disease, but also by the profound social and economic disruption caused by the Conquest.[2]

The Iberian domination of America had a major impact on the indigenous populations, and there is no doubt that the social and economic changes brought about by the Conquest also altered the continent's population dynamics:

- by means of the new diseases and the increased mortality they caused; nonetheless, that influence could not have lasted more than a generation or two as the indigenous populations came to acquire the same sort of immunity as the Europeans;
- by means of the immigration of Europeans and the forced transportation of African slaves that over the course of the sixteenth to nineteenth centuries made net additions of, respectively, 2–3 million and 7–8 million people;[3]
- by means of the racial mixing that ensued, processes that complicate demographic analysis of each of the three groups insofar as they influence one another;
- again as a result of immigration to the new European cities characterized by new social hierarchies relative to the indigenous populations;
- as a result of the population redistribution and concentration carried out by the Spaniards and Portuguese with notable success and aimed at insuring political, religious, and social control;
- by the processes of physical expulsion and dislocation that accompanied the Conquest, especially of marginal ethnicities;
- and by the changes in reproductive regime introduced by Christianization.

These factors had direct and complex influences on the demography of the Americas, demography that many mistakenly believe to have been almost everywhere determined primarily by the increased mortality caused by new diseases. A general reconstruction of the demographic and social history of the continent requires instead that this incomplete vision be superseded and that other factors – some permanent and others transitory – impacting the demographic system of the Indios following contact with Europeans be taken into consideration.

The populations of the Llanos are of course a special case, and no generalization can be made based on their experience. Contact with Europeans was sporadic until the latter half of the seventeenth century. Subsequently, the Jesuits for a time kept them apart from Europeans and Africans so that no *mestizo* or *mulatto* populations developed. But the quantitative information we have for that period is limited. It dates only from the arrival of the Fathers in the region and, given that the Spanish administration took over in 1768 after the expulsion of the Jesuits, covers a period that is brief, demographically speaking. Moreover, compared to the information we have for the thirty missions in Paraguay, the Llanos data is incomplete and less detailed. Nonetheless, the case of the Mojos and other tribes reorganized by the Jesuits is of particular interest, both because effective contact with Europeans came late and because the Jesuits imposed profound modifications on their way of life.

Information on the customs of the Llanos populations comes almost exclusively from the Jesuits, from letters and reports sent to superiors eager to learn about the likelihood of Christianization among them.[4] Some of the early descriptions were repeated (in some cases word for word) in later reports, and it is unclear whether these are cases of laziness or reaffirmations based on additional information. Some cases – for example, the writings of Eguiluz and Altamirano, both provincial superiors who had access to direct sources of information (letters from other Fathers and oral testimonies) – likely conform to the first hypothesis.[5] The issue of coupling and marriage was always at the center of Jesuit interest, in particular promiscuity and the informal way that couples separated and then took on new partners. Among the Guaraní of Paraguay, the Jesuits imposed separate dwellings for each family nucleus in place of their traditional communal huts occupied by multiple family units ("for every cock his own hen house" in the colorful expression of Father Diego de Torres).[6] The Llanos reductions were organized in similar fashion: rectangular buildings (called *cuarteles* or barracks) in which family quarters were carefully divided by walls.[7] In his letter of 1687, Father Orellana described the ease with which couples separated in the land of the Mojos, at the whim of either the woman or the man. Women left their men because "the women do not consider themselves subject to their husbands" and leave them for trifling reasons. The reverse occurred as well, of course, especially in cases of adultery. If a woman left her man while he was away for many days hunting and committed adultery, then either his relatives ("for honor") or hers (because that absence was considered a shirking of responsibility) might seek revenge. Other times, instead, separation might occur,

> for a cross word, for a disparaging phrase, because the wife does not respond to her husband when he speaks to her, or because the husband refuses the drink or food prepared for him by his wife, for jealousy, and for many other trivial reasons; they divorce immediately afterward – and no-one has the authority to stop them – and then each immediately starts looking for a new partner as this people consider the celibate state to be a great hardship.[8]

It was Orellana again who observed that the Fathers had never met Indio men beyond a certain age and still married to their first wives. He does not comment on the reverse situation, but it must have been similar in light of the remarks recorded above. Given the transitory nature of their unions, the marriage rite too was a trifling affair. Among the Baures, whom Altamirano knew well, the Indios

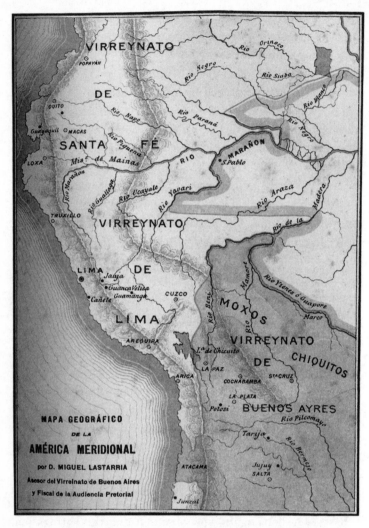

10 Map by Lastarria (end of the eighteenth century)

enter into marriages without any sort of ceremony save that the man buys the daughter from her parents: he pays them with a feathered shield and a string of small pearls that appear to be made of marble and are valued because they come from far away. The *cacique* oversees the contract, and the purchase and the marriage is celebrated by delivering the wife to her husband. And that tie is so loose that sometimes the wife returns to her parents with no better reason than that she is unhappy, and so they simply marry her to someone else.[9]

Father Eder, a Hungarian who lived for thirty years among the Baures, confirmed the lack of ceremony and of any sort of investment in marriage: "And so it happens that the newlyweds contribute their bodies and little more to the marriage, unless you consider a worn out straw mat, a couple of geese or chickens and a few spindles to be a 'dowry,' and from the man a few arrows and a bow." And as for the wedding day,

> it is a sign of their indigence, as there is no sort of banquet, no guests, no celebration, no marking of the marriage at all: the wife goes to the husband's home, carrying a sleeping mat on her back. And then it may happen that without any greeting she enters the home and starts to prepare a meal with the ingredients she has requested, a meal they will eat off the only plate they possess. Each of the spouses will then spend the rest of the day doing what he or she wants, without giving any sign that there has been a wedding.[10]

The criteria used by the young Indios for choosing partners also seemed inscrutable and casual to the Fathers. Poor Father Eder was distressed by the indecision of the betrothed: "It has happened to me many times that those who had freely chosen one another and declared their intention before me, an hour later changed their minds. And not once, but many times, so that I have had to revise the published banns six times in a day."[11] We do know that among the Guaraní the Jesuits were successful in regulating marriages and persuading the young people and their families; the key was to repress promiscuity by enforcing early marriages.

While there was a certain symmetry regarding who decided to end a union (at least until the Jesuits imposed their rules), there was absolute subjugation of the woman within the marriage and an unequal division of labor: "a brutal form of marriage in which the weaker partner, the woman, must carry all the weight while the man enjoys all the comforts."[12]

> It is the woman's job to prepare their drinks and put them into the containers that they use, which are gourds. The men do not work except in the building of huts, in making their weapons, in hunting, fishing, and going to war. The woman carries wood, prepares the food, carries water, weaves the few clothes that they have, and braids the mats and hammocks they use as hanging beds. She tends their garden and raises the children – if you can call raising what amounts to little more than what animals do to insure the survival of the species – though here time is limited by the need to gather the food that is indispensable for their survival.[13]

According to Eder, essential skills for a woman included the ability to prepare *chicha*, toast maize, and weave a new outfit each year for herself and her husband.[14]

Although rare, the Jesuits were insistent in their discouragement of polygamy both among the Mojos and the Baures: "There are few Indios who have two wives, and those who do usually hide the fact," reported Father Áller after his brief stay among the Mojos.[15] Nonetheless, in relation to the founding of the first mission at Loreto, the Fathers "proceeded to separate [the Indios] from their multiple wives so that they would remain with just one, and they won them over with the gift of a knife or some other present, and so they showed themselves to be obedient and docile."[16] In any case, polygamy was infrequent among the Indios, "not out of virtue but of necessity. Because either there are not enough women or they lack the means to maintain them."[17] And although "polygamy was not a minor [vice], nor was it widespread as by the providence of God, there were fewer women than men."[18] In fact, the available data suggest that the disparity was limited; the sex ratio was nearly equal with a few more men than women (about 7–9 percent for the period 1732–48), about what one would expect for a normally constituted population. It is possible of course that there was "competition" for the younger women between younger and older more important men, and that this created the impression that there were few women. Finally, births to unmarried women were rare and much stigmatized; indeed they "were in the habit of tossing these miserable women into the river, bound hand and foot."[19]

Monogamy, indissoluble unions, the isolation of individual family units, and the fight against any sort of promiscuity were the key features of the Fathers' program, the non-negotiable elements for establishment of an ordered society. Initially the Jesuits met with great difficulty, and their general strategy was to concentrate on the very young and so indoctrinate a new generation of good Christians who would follow the accepted precepts of family life. Nor did they have to wait long. Once the Jesuits had received authorization from the adults to take over the task of education, indoctrination of the young took place quickly and, as the Indios formed couples at the age of puberty (a practice encouraged by the Fathers), the first generation of Christian couples came not too long after the founding of the missions. The data, which we examine more below, suggest that the status of adult coincided more or less with that of marriage (and to a lesser extent widowhood). Commenting on the 1831 statistics, Alcides D'Orbigny observed that there were no single males over the age of fourteen nor unmarried females over the age of twelve. "This peculiarity derives from the customs established by the Jesuits who regularly performed marriages for women at age ten and men at age thirteen."[20] A few years after the foundation of Trinidad, Orellana referred to the success they had encouraging monogamy, as "only one Indio male and two or three females, after baptism, have tried to change homes and reject their spouse; prompt punishment, however, has prevented this practice which the others consider impossible."[21] Eder himself wrote that the need to impose order in the area of sexual relations "forced the missionaries not only to tolerate marriages between adolescents, but indeed to encourage marriage once the Indios reach the ages prescribed by the sacred canons [twelve and fourteen] in order to avoid much greater evils."[22]

Early and stable marriage then was a pillar of Jesuit policy and had an impact on fertility as well. The first chroniclers noted particular and interesting characteristics of the reproductive behavior of the Indios, though it is impossible to know how widespread that behavior might have been: "Nothing [. . .] is more horrible than the abominable practice of burying their newborns alive for trifling reasons, at times simply in order to free oneself of the burden of caring for the infant or because it is sickly or difficult."[23] According to other accounts, that barbaric practice was limited to the offspring of mothers who died in childbirth, or else nurslings whose mother died and so they were buried together with her, since it was thought that they would not in any case survive. The same fate awaited one of any pair of twins.[24] These were forms of infanticide linked to a "survival strategy" in which the parental investment in children was limited. There were apparently also superstitions that a woman who miscarried would bring serious illness to the whole village, and in some cases these women were thrown into the river and drowned.[25] The Itonomas were reputed to be highly fertile; and they boiled certain roots in order to prepare a drink that would cure women of sterility. By contrast, the Baures used various herbs as abortifacients as well as mechanical methods (rolling a heavy rock on the woman's belly) to induce miscarriage. The practice of abortion would seem to have been fairly widespread, such that in order to prevent it Father Eder kept a register of pregnant women "so that he could examine them and their fetuses every month and, after nine months, the child they had born."[26]

According to Father Áller, breastfeeding continued till the child was four or five years old.[27] At the same time, the Indios practiced the dangerous feeding practice of giving both cooked and raw fruit to newborns together with mother's milk. Weaning took place when the child rejected the mother's breast

> so that it is usual to see a mother offer one breast to her newborn while a five-year-old suckles on the other! I have also seen a practice considered one of friendship and courtesy between women; when they go visiting or run into a relative or friend, they offer their breasts so that the children of that relative or friend can suckle, and this happens even if they have been a widow or stopped having children for twenty years or more.[28]

Even before the professional demographers, Father D'Orbigny noted that the Mojo women had a lower level of marital fertility than Europeans but higher overall fertility. Lower marital fertility was the result of breastfeeding till the children were three or older "during which period they did not have contact with the men for fear that a new pregnancy would force the mother to wean her child. And so it is rare that a woman have more than five or six children in her lifetime, numbers in any case rarely achieved."[29] D'Orbigny's comments confirm earlier remarks of Eder, according to which there were few women who had as many as five or six children and many instead who had none "even though they were thirty or forty years old and had had several husbands."[30]

The Indios would seem to have had the ability to limit and even control their reproductive behavior. The settlement patterns imposed by the Jesuits instead favored increased fertility because of early, universal, and stable marriage. Those favorable conditions were instead moderated by the reduced fecundity associated with prolonged breastfeeding combined with periods of abstinence and recourse to forms of abortion and infanticide in spite of the Fathers' vigilance. That these populations may have indeed been able to "regulate" fertility emerges from the seasonality of childbearing: more conceptions during the flood season and so more births during the dry season. These are, however, hypotheses at best and, as we shall see, the documentary evidence is scant.

Information on survivorship is even scanter and empirical confirmation more difficult. Certainly indigenous mortality was high, as it was among all populations, European included, living with scarce resources and limited technical knowledge. Life expectancy among the Guaraní, for example, in the Paraguayan missions did not reach twenty-five years even in the periods not struck by epidemics.[31] Scientific research has discounted the myth according to which pre-Columbian populations in the Americas (i.e., before contact) were long-lived and free of infectious diseases. Contemporary observations, however, seem to contradict one another. Few Indios reached the age of sixty, but little was noted in the way of serious or debilitating diseases. Likely the explanation lies in the European perception of the Indios' ability to withstand deprivation, physical pain, and illness as a sign of good health. Europeans in fact marveled at the natives' tranquil acceptance of death. According to Eder:

> Certainly the Indios suffer from many fewer diseases than the Europeans. They would, for example, not have small pox at all [with which Eder had been afflicted] except that the Spaniards brought it here in recent years and it nearly wiped out two of the reductions. Other unknown diseases include apoplexy, kidney stones, hemorrhoids, leprosy, syphilis and many others. By contrast, the diseases that afflict them the most include dysentery, pleurisy, fevers, catarrh, all sorts of tumors and abscesses; and finally and above all, worms, which carry most to their graves.

These latter diseases certainly suffice to explain a high level of mortality. And it is worth asking to what degree the concentration into villages of populations that had formerly been broadly spread out might have influenced mortality. One can imagine that it caused an increase in dysentery from the contamination of water and food caused by garbage and human excrement; and all things being equal it could have increased the risk of infectious diseases, both endemic ones and those introduced from outside. On the other hand, the more sedentary life in the missions, the discouragement of hunting, a more varied and stable diet, and the help offered by the Jesuits may have moderated other mortality factors. In 1713 Father Messia reported that the Fathers visited the sick twice a day, accompanied by the nurses, and brought meat to all of them and lessened their ills "using those medicines they could get from the earth and others brought from outside; and of course they administered the sacraments which the sick cried out for even before there was real danger." It is pointless, though, to attempt to evaluate the relative importance of these factors based on purely theoretical considerations.[32]

The largest question mark regards the introduction of new viral diseases, especially smallpox. We know that Santa Cruz de la Sierra was struck by the pandemic of 1590 that swept through all of South America. But did it also spread to the Llanos, a geographically isolated region with only sporadic contact with the Spanish and characterized by the sort of humid clime that does not favor the transmission of viruses? And when subsequently might we date epidemics? The thirty Paraguayan missions and the surrounding area suffered smallpox epidemics in 1695, 1718–19, 1733–9, 1749 (maybe), and 1764–5, one every fourteen to eighteen years.[33] The isolation of the Llanos populations was much greater than that of the people who lived along the banks of the Paraná and Uruguay rivers, exposed as they were to frequent contact with the Spaniards and enjoying a much more favorable environment. Other than Eder, our information is sporadic. And Eder himself is contradicted by the experience of the Concepción Mission – the first among the Baures and founded in 1708 – recounted by Altamirano. Its foundation was made difficult when a pestilence broke out in the new village: "it began with catarrh and developed into dangerous pains on the flanks before exploding into a general and horrible outbreak of smallpox as they lacked any defense; our missionaries were busy day and night, caring for the sick, baptizing the children, and preparing the adults for baptism."[34] Orellana instead refers to a *peste de viruelas* that broke out around 1680, though deaths were apparently few thanks to the care administered by the Fathers (an unlikely claim); moreover, he had been told about other epidemics that had wiped out entire villages which survived in name only. But these are references to the pre-missionary period, and the accounts blur together facts, names, and hearsay.[35]

We get further testimony from the governor of Santa Cruz de la Sierra, Argamoza, in his 1737 report to the king on the Mojo missions and their 35,000 inhabitants. In that land, flooded for several months of the year, "there are many who are sick, and rare is the year in which some pestilence does not strike all the villages. There have been epidemics so strong as to claim 1,200 lives in just two reductions."[36] Moreover, the cold winds that blow down from the Peruvian Cordillera (the *surazos*) and follow suddenly on oppressive heat caused other epidemics. Argamoza does not make explicit reference to smallpox, though it is possible that the terrible epidemics that struck Paraguay in the mid-1630s also spread to Chaco and the Llanos. D'Orbigny's references come instead from the 1820s and 1830s, more than half a century after the expulsion of the Jesuits and establishment of a Spanish civil administration. In terms of pathology, then, this was the period of integration with the rest of the region. Smallpox nearly tripled the normal number of deaths in 1831. "The extraordinary mortality suffered by the Mojos derives from two sources: either the cold that is so devastating for the children or from one of the many fevers – smallpox, measles, and scarlet fever – that massacre people of all ages." Moreover, the practice of bathing to ease the terrible burning that accompanied cases of smallpox or measles only worsened the consequences.[37] Higher mortality among the men can be attributed to their different lifestyle compared to women and frequent accidents during navigation in the flood months. Nonetheless, mortality was highest in the dry months (May–July), when the coldest winds blow, especially among children suffering from respiratory ailments. The fact of very high infant mortality finds confirmation from another Father who in 1711 referred to the "certain fruit that heaven gathers from this mission in the form of nearly one thousand children who die before the age of reason and are noted down in the registers of deaths from each reduction."[38]

The *planillas* (or *catálogos* or statistical prospects) that recapitulate the population of the various missions at the end of a particular year offer few details useful for demographic analysis and cover relatively few years.[39] From them we can learn the total population divided into baptized and "*catecumenos*" (or non-baptized), who were particularly numerous in the early phase of the missions; and the number of *casados* or more precisely the number of conjugal couples or families.

In general, one can distinguish the *niños* and the *niñas* (or also *parvulos* or *pueri*), though it is difficult to attach a precise age range to these terms; they should go up to the age of first communion and so between seven and ten years, though the context suggests that the age of marriage (under twelve or fourteen years for example) may be more likely. We also find the category of *viudos* (widows), though not always (not in 1713 or 1720); and in those latter cases we do not know to which category they were assigned (married or unmarried). Finally, the category of *solutos* or *mancebos* refers to sexually mature individuals who are not yet married.

Table A.1 includes various measures for the period 1713–1831. The data for 1713, which differ dramatically from those for the other dates, lack demographic significance; conversion of the Baures was in its initial phase and the number of non-baptized was high.[40] The latter, even if joined as a couple and with children, were not classified as *casados*, so that the *casados* were badly underestimated and constituted a small percentage of the population. Between 1720 and 1831 the indices have a certain stability and permit some observations. There are on average four persons for every conjugal couple (family), a level below that prevalent among the Guaraní in Paraguay where between 1690 and

1767 that index stood between four and five. The proportion of spouses among the entire population is about 50 percent and so significantly above the Guaraní figure of 45 percent. Finally, the number of children per couple is significantly lower in the Llanos than in Paraguay. At the same time, it is possible that the two groups of Jesuits used different age ranges to define children, and so any interpretation of these differences remains ambiguous.

The *planillas* for 1732, 1736, and 1748 all use the same nomenclature and come from the period in which the missions were well established (see map 11). A few significant figures are included in table A.2 which distinguishes between the three regions of Mojos, Baures, and the Pampas. Doubt remains as to whether or not the variations revealed in the table might be produced by the way the Indios were categorized, and there is really no way to resolve that uncertainty given the data available. Who exactly were the unmarried? What was their minimum age? Did that age coincide with the maximum age for "children"? Is it justified, as is done in the table, to consider "adults" as the difference between total population and children? Keeping these reservations in mind, we can nonetheless hazard a few observations. The first is that the smaller average size of families, the lower ratio between children and married, and the higher proportion of widows in 1732 could be the result of a demographic crisis in that year or the years immediately preceding. The second is that Baures displays a consistently more solid demographic system – higher ratios of children to married and persons per family – than the Pampas, one closer to the levels among the Guaraní of Paraguay. Moreover, between 1732 and 1748, the Baures population grew slowly (from 13,743 to 14,518) while the Pampas one declined (from 8,757 to 4,924). However, we do not know to what degree these changes are the result of migration, dispersion, and re-composition

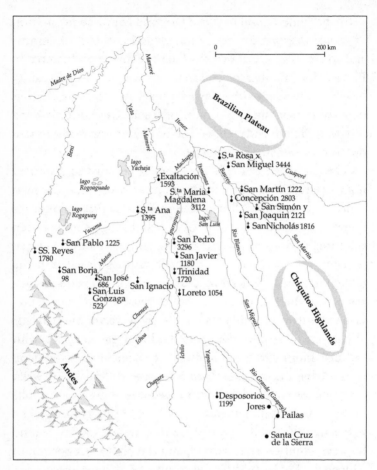

11 Population of the missions of the Llanos de Mojos in 1748

as opposed to factors of mortality and reproduction. A third observation regards the male to female ratio, both among children and the total population. In both cases there is a notable (though not abnormal) excess of males: 113 percent among the children and 108 percent among the total population. There are several possible interpretations: a failure to count girls (as frequently happens, even today, in developing

countries), greater mortality for girls (differential infanticide), or a higher age limit for boys than girls as a function of
puberty. Unfortunately there is no way to know which might
be closer to the truth.

D'Orbigny gathered population data for the Llanos
during the years 1828–31 (table A.3) that reveal three similarities with the Guaraní of Paraguay. The first is the serious
mortality crisis caused by the smallpox epidemic of 1831;
during that year deaths were two and a half times greater
than the average for the three years previous. Since smallpox surely struck during the eighteenth century as well, we
are dealing with a non-"virgin" population that has been
largely immunized; not endemic, the virus was reintroduced
from outside the region and broke out in an epidemic when
it found enough "fuel" there. The fuel was population born
after the last epidemic; and after fifteen years that population constituted about half of the total. That interval was
in fact the average for smallpox outbreaks in eighteenth-
century America. The 1831 epidemic wiped out one Indio in
eight during a single year, but the high natality of 1828–30,
untroubled by crisis mortality, produced an excess of births
relative to deaths (1,416) adequate to compensate for the
excess of deaths relative to births in 1831 (1,413). Among
the Guaraní of Paraguay, average natality (61 per thousand)
and mortality (44 per thousand) over the period 1690–1767
was similar to that in the Llanos for 1828–30. These data
amply confirm D'Orbigny's observation that legitimate fertility (namely among married women) was relatively low, but
universal and early marriage (and so a high percentage of
adult married women) more than compensated for the low
number of children per married woman and so generated a
high level of overall fertility (births per total population).[41]

The available data do not allow us to determine whether
the demographic system of the Llanos was unique or similar

to that of other indigenous populations. Certainly the fact
of early and universal marriage encouraged by the Jesuits
created the potential for rapid growth, even given the high
levels of mortality suffered by the Indios, growth that should
have been adequate to offset periodic crises. That potential,
however, was not fully realized thanks to fertility-limiting
practices, described by the Fathers, that included extended
periods of breastfeeding (and so long inter-birth intervals),
sexual taboos during those periods, and one form or another
of abortion and infanticide. We are not able, however, to
understand how these reproductive strategies interacted
with the fragile ecology of the Llanos, namely the limited
supply of cultivable land and the precarious nature of the
settlements.[42]

The history of the Llanos population can be divided into
five phases (see figure A.1): first, one of growth until the mission system reached maturity around 1720; then about forty
years of stability; a decade of rapid decline (1760–70) that
included conflict with the Portuguese and expulsion of the
Jesuits; and another sixty years of stability (1770–1830). The
fifth period of disastrous decline culminated in the final third
of the nineteenth century when the rubber boom attracted
migration to the Amazon forest. Those long phases of stability seem to suggest that in periods not disrupted by external
events, the demographic system managed to make up the
losses suffered in crisis periods with a good excess of births
over deaths in the years free of epidemics. Moreover, after
1720, the migratory phase of the missions – characterized by
a high proportion of non-baptized *catecumenos* – must have
declined rapidly.[43] We do not know, however, how many
Indios might have subsequently left the missions to return to
a traditional way of life.

The population counted at the end of 1768 – the year of
the Jesuit *extranamiento* – was under 19,000; that of 1752

(the most recent preceding count) over 31,000. What happened in between to cause this rapid decline? Tension and conflict between the Spaniards and Portuguese surely played an important role. That conflict derived from the *Tratado de Limites* signed in 1750 and establishing the boundaries between Spanish and Portuguese territory; to the east, the border between the Mato Grosso and the Mojo province was fixed along the Guaporé river.

Although it had not led to open hostility, Brazilian pressure on the land of the Mojos had been apparent for some time, from exploratory expeditions and from the attempts to establish commercial relations and to control and intercept, or in any case exploit, the traffic between the Atlantic coast and Alto Perú. That pressure became explicit with the discovery of gold on the banks of the Cuiabá river in Brazil in 1718, the creation of the Capitanía of Mato Grosso in 1748, and the foundation, on the Spanish side, of missions among the Chiquitos which became targets for raids by the Brazilian *bandeirantes*.[44]

In partial observance of the *Tratado de Limites*, the Fathers began dismantling the San Miguel and Santa Rosa missions on the Portuguese side of the Guaporé; they intended to hand them over definitively once the Portuguese had fulfilled the other conditions imposed by the agreement. Then in 1760, the governor of Mato Grosso, Rollín, decided to occupy Santa Rosa "violently taking possession of the land and the buildings [. . .] with the intention of occupying them permanently and continuing the pillaging they had begun and which severely injured the Indios who farmed those lands."[45] The Portuguese had also crossed the river and captured half of the Indios in the new mission of Santa Rosa, "taking away the Indian women in order to force the men to come. In anticipation of a possible armed conflict, the president of the Audiencia de Charcas had asked the provincial of Perú for information on the strength of the missions, the resources available, the men in arms, transport capabilities, and other things." According to the response, there were "4,000 *hombres de flecha*" in the seventeen missions, though only about half of these were available as the others were needed for normal agricultural and transportation work. The missions could supply about fifty large canoes with twenty Indios each and a similar number of small canoes. With regard to foodstuffs, there was enough "to support soldiers, but not for very long."[46] In the meantime, the *Tratado* had been nullified as Portugal and Spain took opposite sides in the Seven Years War, and the continued presence of Portuguese in areas previously held by the Spanish led to open conflict in 1763. The Portuguese attacked and burned the San Miguel mission, taking away the Indios as prisoners. They also attacked Santa Rosa which put up resistance. Meanwhile, a large Spanish expedition with Indio auxiliaries moved slowly toward the Mojos, but was forced to withdraw when the rainy season began. The next year a second expedition was organized under the command of Juan de Pestaña, president of the Audiencia de Charcas; but when the troops finally gathered at San Pedro (home of the Father superior of the missions) in April 1766, they were decimated by fevers and desertions and so unable to carry out a decisive attack against the Portuguese positions.[47] Meanwhile an agreement had been reached between the Portuguese and the Spanish, and the conflict ended. As in many other cases, the negative effect of the conflict was not so much deaths in battle, but owing to the disruption of social and economic equilibria. The Indios paid a high price:

> The Luso-Hispanic struggle turned all of Moxos into a theater of war. Even those missions not threatened by Portuguese arms felt the effect of the conflict. Resources of food and animals, slowly accumulated over the years,

quickly disappeared in supplying the Spanish cause. Large numbers of neophytes were redirected from their tasks to carry, build, and fight.[48]

Many fields were abandoned, and the Mojos suffered deprivations similar to those that afflicted the Paraguayan Guaraní during the rebellion of the *comuneros* in the 1730s and the conflict with the Portuguese in the 1760s.[49]

A period of recovery normally follows each external shock – wars, epidemics, other catastrophes – as demographic equilibrium is re-established and social and economic life returns to normal. On 27 February, 1767, instead, Charles III ordered the expulsion of the Jesuits from Spain and her American colonies. In May of 1768, the twenty-four Jesuits of the missions were gathered together at San Pedro and escorted first to Santa Cruz and then to Cochabamba, Oruro, Tacna, and Arica, and then by sea to Lima whence they departed for Europe. Only fourteen of them made it to Lima, the others having died during the voyage.[50] The expulsion signaled the end of an era, one characterized by social and demographic isolation, and opened the way to the colonists of Santa Cruz who did not hesitate to exploit the population of the Llanos. It also led to the replacement of the theocratic government of the Fathers with a civil government and normal clergy who proved to be incompetent, if not corrupt. That time, there was no recovery following the shock.

EPILOG

In less than a century, the work of the Jesuits had profoundly changed the society of the Llanos de Mojos. Conversion of the Indios was the central feature of that change, and it marked completion of a spiritual mission that found adepts who were both fervent and easily manipulated by the Fathers. The material impact was equally radical as their prior dispersion and semi-nomadism were replaced and regimented by a network of mission villages. New livestock and crops increased available resources and reduced their dependence on hunting. They acquired new technical skills in agriculture and in the working of textiles, metal, and wood. The rules of cohabitation were rewritten along more prudent lines, and new Christian customs profoundly changed familial organization. Jesuit government also protected the Indios from the danger of enslavement by Spanish colonists or Portuguese *bandeiras* and in any case from being constrained to function as servants to the Spanish of Santa Cruz. Strict segregation from Europeans and Africans prevented any sort of miscegenation, while the Llanos network of missions, together with that established in bordering Chiquitania, also served an important political function as it helped to block commercial and military penetration by the Portuguese.

While the destructive impact of contact with the Europeans was much attenuated for the Indios of the Llanos – in contrast to experience in many other parts of the Americas – no barrier succeeded in protecting them from the Eurasian pathogens that those same Europeans unknowingly brought along with them. Smallpox had already struck the Indios in the vicinity of Santa Cruz de la Sierra around 1590, as contemporary accounts attest, though it is doubtful that it made its way to the damp, remote, and isolated region of the Llanos till the beginning of the Jesuit period. Beginning in the late seventeenth century, instead, smallpox and similar viral infections were repeatedly introduced from outside the region with disastrous consequences – as always in such cases – for a society like the Mojos characterized by rapid demographic turnover and very high natality. Nonetheless, the population remained stable for four decades, until the Luso–Hispanic conflict and the expulsion of the Jesuits: early, universal, and stable marriage combined with that very high natality to fill in the gaps.

After 1768 mission society broke down, much as happened with the missions in Paraguay and other parts of the continent. Just the same, and contrary to the experience in Paraguay, where the departure of the Jesuits led to the disintegration of the network of settlement, in the Llanos the present-day population distribution of the Beni Department still follows that laid down in the eighteenth century. The layout of the reductions followed the grid system used throughout Hispanic America and adapted to the Jesuit model. In 1742 a Portuguese traveler described the Magdalena mission, surrounded by a wall of adobe with a large church dominating the main plaza, in the following way:

The great square, according to the usual style of these Jesuit establishments, had a cross in the centre; but in other aspects, the ground plan appears to have been traced by some whimsical architect for in whatever direction the houses were seen, they appeared in regular order, like the chequeres of a chess-board, and the country was laid out in regular order with white paths of sand. A considerable space was enclosed within the walls, so as to afford room for folds and gardens; and the settlement bore the marks of civilization: there were shops for weavers, carpenters, and carvers; an *engenho* [mill], where rum as well as sugar was made; public kitchens and stocks for the enforcement of wholesome discipline."[1]

In Father Eder's mission, the dwellings (which housed two or three independent families) were 24 *varas* long, 13 wide, and 10 to the top of the roof (19.4 × 10.5 × 8.1 meters) including porticoes of 2½ *varas* each on the long sides, leaving each family an enclosed space of 40–60 square meters. The walls of clay and mud were whitewashed.[2] The churches were imposing, almost always consisting of three naves, and decorated by the natives. In Father Eder's mission, the church faced on to a plaza each side of which measured 70 paces and in each corner of which sat a small chapel. Given the lack of stone in the Llanos – as with the missions of Paraguay – these structures were supported by tall pillars made from trees brought down from the slopes of the Andes. Religious instruction, to which all children under twelve were subject without exception, took place near the church and the house of the Fathers. The children had to attend morning Mass and evening prayers and catechism. In school they learned music and singing as well as reading and writing.[3] The economic activity of the missions increased and diversified, promoting a rudimentary division of labor, thanks to instruction in new crafts and the availability of iron and steel tools. As a result, a two-tier society emerged: the *familia* consisted of notables, technicians, and artisans, while the *pueblo* was made up of those who worked the land and carried out other menial tasks. The raising of livestock – derived from the few dozen animals that Father Barace had with great audacity brought from Santa Cruz at the end of the seventeenth century – had taken hold so that by the mid-eighteenth century the missions' *estancias* included 54,345 head of cattle and 26,317 horses.[4] The success of the *estancias* assured a regular supply of meat to the missions, "reducing hunting and fishing to simple pastimes" and freeing up a vast quantity of labor for artisan work.[5] The bishop of Santa Cruz claimed that livestock raising guaranteed "the survival of the villages, because if [the Indios] did not have meat, they would devise ways to capture monkeys, parrots, and anything else they can bring down with their arrows, and so they would live apart, without government or doctrine, as was the practice among the infidels."[6] The Jesuits had introduced rice and cocoa and improved and expanded the cultivation of sugar cane, cotton, and maize.[7] At the beginning of the eighteenth century, the territorial limits of the missions were established, defining where each should farm and raise its animals; those areas normally corresponded with the ones previously occupied by the ethnicities that entered into the mission. Each mission also had its *chacra del cura* (field of the Fathers) that the Indios farmed to supply food for the Fathers but also, and above all, for the needs of the collectivity: for the sick and disabled; for those unable to extract sufficient resources from their allotment; to provide reserves against periods of scarcity; and to produce goods for sale and so generate the income needed to buy the tools and manufactures that could not be produced by the missions themselves.[8] Their few exports passed through Santa Cruz de la Sierra and were sold in Alto Perú

by means of Jesuit intermediaries in La Plata, Oruro, Potosí,
Cochabamba, and La Paz. The Jesuit college in Lima fur-
nished imports needed from Europe.[9] Agricultural concerns
owned by the Jesuits in Alto Perú supplied oil, wine, and
flour.[10]

It is impossible to measure how much governance by
the Jesuits changed the lives of the Indios compared to the
period before the missions, but it is reasonable to conclude
that they enjoyed a number of improvements: more comfort-
able dwellings, a more varied diet thanks to the introduction
of new crops, higher productivity thanks to the introduction
of a division of labor and European tools, greater security
thanks to fewer conflicts (with the notable exception of the
Luso–Hispanic War and the negative impact we discussed
above) and protection against raids and exploitation (though
here one would have to make a comparison with the period
before the arrival of any Europeans at all), and improved
technical knowledge. Certainly the Fathers created a system
closed to the outside world (Spaniards were forbidden from
living in the villages), depending on strictly enforced rules,
and sure of the obedience of its subjects; and one relying on
an autarchic and parsimonious economy and a vast territory.
Ultimately, the expulsion of the Jesuits in 1768 eroded this
system of social and civil order and opened it to the outside
world.

It is commonly held that the situation of the Indios dete-
riorated in the decades after the expulsion of the Jesuits;
and there is solid evidence to that effect in the religious,
civil, and socioeconomic realms. Nonetheless, the population remained stable, varying between about 20,000 the
year before the Jesuits left (1767) and 23,000 in 1831; the
data gathered by D'Orbigny for 1828–31, just a few years
after Bolivian independence (1825), reveal a solid demographic system still based on early, universal marriage and

very high natality.[11] Nonetheless, the network of settlement
must have contracted to some extent due to the decline
and dispersal of several missions, the populations of which
were normally incorporated into others. While one new
mission was founded in 1792 (San Ramón absorbing population from Magdalena), four others were abandoned (San
José, San Borja, San Simón, and San Martín). Santa Rosa
meanwhile had been transferred to the other side of the Rio
Iténez under the authority of Jesuits in Brazilian territory.
In the mid-1780s, Exaltación was in decline and many families from there were migrating to Portuguese dominions.[12]
In 1775 San Javier was incorporated into Trinidad following
a flood.[13] During that long period, Mojo society continued
to function more or less along the lines laid down by the
Fathers, though their rules underwent some severe distor-
tions. Following departure of the Jesuits, the bishop of Santa
Cruz de la Sierra, Francisco Ramón Herboso, issued a regu-
lation, approved by the Audiencia de Charcas, that ordered
preservation of the Jesuit institutions and substitution of the
Fathers with secular clergy (*curas*). The residents of Santa
Cruz were authorized to trade with the Mojos, and anything
produced by the communal system in excess of the missions'
immediate needs continued to be handled by the monopoly.
The proceeds, however, went into the treasuries of Santa
Cruz and Chuquisaca. Government by the *curas* continued
undisturbed till 1788 and showed itself to be a disaster both
for incompetence and corruption. Many of the *curas* were
not ordained priests:

> Herboso's original contingent was in many ways typical of
> the entire body of Jesuit replacements. Of the six, only one
> man, Antonio Peñalosa, was an ordained priest. The others,
> enumerated in the documents as *curas doctrineros*, were either
> seminarians, incomplete in their spiritual preparation, or

laymen. Of the 55 men who served in the missions between 1767 and 1790, only 22 (40%) were ordained priests.[14]

Complaints about their misgovernment began almost immediately, during the governorship of Aymerich who lamented their lack of vocation: "They are forced to come here and do not dedicate themselves to these farms with any sense of duty but instead hope only to leave [. . .]. They do not learn the language, and I doubt that the villages produce even a quarter of what they did before."[15] Nonetheless, they quickly learned to pursue their own interests and inspired scandal with their irregular and promiscuous behavior. Governor Lázaro de Ribera engaged in a bitter struggle to reform the missions of which much evidence survives, including a letter to the king accompanied by voluminous documentation relative to a meeting with the bishop of Santa Cruz de la Sierra who was accused of covering up the misdeeds of the *curas*:

> Can it possibly be tolerated that the most illustrious bishop, rather than visiting those lands to pacify his flock, stays instead at a distance of 150 leagues, railing against those who attempt to do their duty and seeking to cover up the hateful tracks of a number of priests whose promiscuity, thieving, smuggling, cruelty, crimes, and excesses know no bounds? [. . .] Can your pity contemplate the abandoned villages, the sacked churches, the Indios treated with shocking cruelty and so severely oppressed that they cannot count on the security of their wives and their daughters, unhappy victims of the irregularity and impudence of these priests?[16]

It could be that the new governor was carried away by the vigor of his own rhetoric. Nonetheless, other data speak clearly: in the six years prior to the arrival of Ribera the annual earning extracted from the missions amounted to 8,500 pesos per year as compared to an average of 46,000 during the first two years of his administration (thanks to the repression of corruption).[17] Ribera's effort at reform succeeded in separating the spiritual administration from the civil one, but did not accomplish lasting improvements. In fact, those reforms had an unintended and perverse effect, "as the Indios now found themselves more enslaved than previously, and rather than having just one absolute master, they had two whose continuous disagreements and poor conduct accelerated the descent of the missions into rack and ruin."[18]

From an economic standpoint, the Jesuit period enjoyed a degree of success in the production of candles, cocoa, and cotton. Wax for candles and soap was derived from fat obtained during the butchering of livestock. Under the new regime, candle production entered into crisis because of the depletion of the herd. The production of cocoa and cotton (which became the basis for manufacturing indigenous textiles) instead increased. These goods were exported to Alto Perú, though there is proof that much of it made its way to Brazil as contraband.[19] The emphasis on exports pursued by the post-Jesuit administration worked to the detriment of traditional practices, especially agriculture which was shifted to fields farther from the missions, a move that increased the workload of the Indios. The fruits of their labors, once carefully redistributed by the Jesuits, were now commandeered by intermediaries and smugglers. In the final years of their government, the Jesuits generated 60,000 pesos per year through commerce with their representatives as compared to less than half that by their successors around 1830. In that latter period, Governor Carmelo Rivera systematically checked the canoes used to transport the exported goods and discovered that a large portion of them were being illicitly withheld by administrators (who were immediately sacked).[20]

Three-quarters of a century after the expulsion of the Jesuits, in 1842, both the theocracy and the monopoly that had survived them came to an end when the whole region became part of Bolivia as the Beni Department. The number of ethnic European residents, who had already begun to settle in the region after 1768, increased. Some came in search of the phantom wealth of the Jesuits – in fact they left behind little more than the accumulated stock for export and the furnishings of the churches – while others, noted above, came as *curas doctrineros* or as part of their entourage; and others still for trade or smuggling. The isolation of the region had, in any case, come to an end:

> The relative ethnological unity of the region from the Jesuit era was broken, and the doors were open to the mixing of races and castes with their diverse and conflicting energies. One can say that from that point forward, Alto Perú expanded to Mojos. The missionary province entered into and became progressively more a part of the general Bolivian confusion.[21]

Some Indios from the region also migrated to Santa Cruz to work for the Spaniards, and the general process of mixing accelerated after 1842:

> It often happened that people of various extractions attached themselves to the retinue of prefects who were appointed to the brand-new district and generally chosen from among the notables of Santa Cruz [. . .] Nor was it rare that well-to-do individuals, whole families, and masters and their workers follow that same path with the intention of investing their modest capital in the raising of livestock on the fertile fields along the Mamoré, Yacuma, and Baures Rivers.[22]

Unfortunately, the absence of quantitative data makes it impossible to know either the scale of the European presence or the degree of racial mixing. Both were likely small given the remoteness, poverty, and isolation of the Llanos.

In the second half of the nineteenth century, the population of the Llanos experienced a crisis that brought it to the verge of extinction. The central figure in this crisis was a tree commonly found in the Amazon forest and referred to by botanists as *Hevea brasiliensis*. Antonio de Herrera marveled at the beginning of the seventeenth century: "There are trees that when they are cut shed milky tears that can be converted into white rubber."[23] That tree and those tears became a precious commodity after Goodyear discovered the vulcanization process and the many uses of rubber for an industrializing society became apparent. The Brazilians began to exploit the rubber trees (or *siringa*) in their forests, working their way up the Amazon to where it is joined by the Madeira and then up that major tributary as well. That area belonged at the time to Bolivia, and there were already a few cattle raisers there from Santa Cruz. At the beginning of the 1860s the Brazilian explorers (*siringueros*) were followed into that region by their Bolivian counterparts.[24] As demand for rubber grew, a steady stream of migration flowed from the Llanos to the banks of the Madeira. In 1867 Brazilian diplomats sought to acquire this area of promising resources, over which Bolivia had legal sovereignty but scant control, and successfully obtained 300,000 square kilometers, an area the size of Italy and including both sides of the Madeira up to where it is joined by the Beni and Mamoré, for a modest fee.[25] The Englishman Edward Mathews carried out a careful study, according to which in 1873 forty-three canoes carrying merchants of cinchona bark and rubber speculators traveled down the rapids of the Madeira from the Llanos, while only thirteen made the return trip:

We may average the Indians that leave Bolivia with these canoes at ten per canoe, and thus we have an exodus of 430 Indians from their country in twelve months while only 130 return in the same period; we thus have 300 Indians lost to Bolivia in 1873, and as the rubber-collecting fever has been decidedly on the decrease for the last four or five years, the year 1873 does not give a fifth of the number of Indians that have left in previous years. We may, I venture to think, estimate the drain of human life that the department of Beni has suffered from the Northern Brazilian rubber trade at 1,000 men per annum during the decade of 1862 to 1872.

The female to male ratio at that time was five to one, while according to Mathews the total population had shrunk to 8,000.[26] And as the men were essentially used up, women too were recruited for rubber work. Meanwhile the Indios were at the mercy of their Brazilian employers; falling into debt, they found themselves in a state of semi-slavery, decimated as well by alcohol and disease. In 1874, the village of Carmen counted 750 women and fifteen men; the Indios were supplied to the Brazilian merchants by corrupt local officials who received a payoff for every laborer supplied.[27]

So ends our story. We do not know if prior to the arrival of the Spaniards the populations of the Llanos lived in stable and peaceful societies. There were certainly conflicts, and violent ones, over land. We do know that the arrival of the Europeans, first in the vain search for El Dorado and then in the seventeenth century to seize Indios for slave-like labor, administered a severe shock to the local populations; that it was not lethal owes much to the distance and isolation of the region which made expeditions there costly and rare. The raids were specifically condemned by the Laws of the Indies, but those laws were conceived thousands of miles away and their enforcement in the vast regions east of the Andes was practically nil. Then, in less than a century, the Jesuits succeeded in establishing a different organization, drawing the indigenous societies with a minimum of trauma into a new Christian, ordered, and peaceful world. Necessary conditions for that success were complete isolation and absolute control. Following their expulsion and opening of the region to the outside world – a relative opening given the geographical isolation and long distances involved – that organization survived with a few changes nearly to the middle of the nineteenth century. Its foundations, however, gradually eroded and collapsed completely when the echoes of industrialization reached to the upper Amazon, initiating a new and degrading form of servitude that nearly brought about the society's extinction. Fortunately, that extinction was avoided and the Mojo language is still spoken in some parts of the Llanos. The demographic system – the complex interplay of survival, unions, reproduction, and mobility – was presumably strengthened in the world created by the Jesuits. A rational network of settlements created larger and more efficient communities; mobility was controlled and minimized; and unions became stable and universally established at young ages. That system was able to withstand the shock of new Eurasian diseases and maintain its dimensions. It was instead the political and economic shocks that brought about demographic disruption: the Luso–Hispanic War at the end of the Jesuit period and the migration caused by rubber-prospecting a century later. In demographic terms, the Llanos suffered more from attacks by humans than from attacks by microbes.

CHRONOLOGY

1513   On 25 September Vasco Núñez Balboa crosses the isthmus of Panama and arrives at the Mar del Sur (Pacific Ocean)

1519–56 Reign of Charles V

1524–5   First voyage of Francisco Pizarro along the Pacific coast

1526–7   Francisco Pizarro's second voyage with a stay on Gallo Island

1529   On 26 July Pizarro is recognized as having discovered Perú

1530   On 27 December Pizarro sets off from Panama on his third voyage

1531–8   Alfinger, Espira, and Federman, representatives of the Welser bankers, lead expeditions from Coro (Venezuela) to the Orinoco and Amazon basins

1532   On 16 May Pizarro advances into the Incan Empire from Tumbez

1532	On 16 November Pizarro captures Atahuallpa at Cajamarca
1533	From 13 May to 25 July, the gold and silver ransom for Atahuallpa is melted down and distributed among Pizarro's men
1533	On 26 July Atahuallpa is executed
1533	On 15 November Pizarro enters Cuzco
1534	Sebastián de Benalcázar marches on Quito
1535–7	Expedition of Diego de Almagro to Chile
1536	On 6 January Pizarro founds Los Reyes (Lima)
1536	Incan rebellion and siege of Cuzco
1537	Foundation of Asunción (Paraguay) by Juan de Ayolas
1536–8	Gonzalo Jiménez de Quesada's expedition leaves Santa Marta on 5 April, 1536; foundation of Santa Fe (Bogotá) on 6 August, 1538, capital of the Reina de Nueva Granada (present-day Colombia)
1538	On 26 April Hernando Pizarro defeats Almagro in the Battle of Las Salinas
1538	Execution of Almagro on 8 July
1538	Quesada, Benalcázar, and Federman meet up on the *sabana* of Bogotá
1538	Pedro de Candía's expedition from Cuzco over the Andes; the survivors join with Peranzures
1540	Pedro de Valdivia's expedition to conquer Chile
1540	Pope Paul III formally approves the Company of Jesus
1541	On 26 July the followers of Almagro kill Francisco Pizarro
1541	Felipe de Utre's expedition from Coro
1541–2	Gonzal Pizarro's disastrous expedition from Quito over the Andes; in November, 1541, Orellana and fifty-seven companions begin navigation of the

Napo, Coca, and Amazon rivers; they arrive at the island of Cubagua (Venezuela) on 11 September, 1542

1542   On 16 September Almagro the Younger and the followers of Almagro are defeated in the Battle of Chupas

1545   Silver discovered in the *cerro* of Potosí

1548   Pedro de la Gasca defeats Gonzalo Pizarro in the Battle of Jaquijaguana; Gonzalo is executed and his rebellion put down

1551   First council at Lima

1554   On 8 October Hernández Girón's uprising is defeated in the Battle of Pucará; the civil war is over

1556   Abdication of Charles V; coronation of Philip II

1556   Death of St. Ignatius Loyola

1558–60 Ñuflo de Chaves's expedition from Asunción to the land of the Xarayes, the Chiquitos, and the Mojos

1559   Creation of the Audiencia de Charcas (present-day Bolivia)

1561   On 26 February Ñuflo de Chaves founds Santa Cruz de la Sierra

1563   Creation of the Audiencia de Quito (present-day Ecuador)

1568   Arrival of the Jesuits in Perú

1568–9 Juan Álvarez Maldonado's expedition from Cuzco across the Andes to the Madre de Dios basin

1569–81 Administration of Francisco de Toledo, fifth viceroy of Perú

1570–3 Toledo's *Visita general*; forced transfer of the Indios to planned villages

1572   War in Villacamba and execution of Tupac Amaru

1573	Royal decree assigns *descubrimiento* of the Mojos to the colonists of Santa Cruz de la Sierra
1587	Arrival of the first Jesuits in Santa Cruz de la Sierra
1595	Expedition led by the governor of Santa Cruz, Figueroa, into the land of the Mojos as far as the upper Mamoré
1602	Mendoza Mate de Luna's expedition into the land of the Mojos
1609	Founding of the Paraguayan missions begins
1617	Solís de Holguín's expedition into the land of the Mojos
1625	Founding of the missions in the Llanos of the Meta and Casanare rivers (Orinoco) begins
1637	Founding of the Mayanas missions, on the banks of the Marañón and Ucayali rivers, begins
1667	de Ampuero's expedition among the Mojos, for exploration and slaves, accompanied by Confrere Juan de Soto
1668–9	Vain attempts at conversion by Fathers Bermudo and Áller and Confrere de Soto
1675	Lima authorizes the beginning of missionary work among the Mojos; Fathers Marbán and Barace and Confrere del Castillo set out
1682	Foundation of Nuestra Señora de Loreto, first mission among the Mojos
1686	Foundation of Santísima Trinidad, second mission among the Mojos (today capital city of the Beni Department)
1700–1	Provincial Diego Francisco Altamirano visits the Mojos missions
1702	On 16 September Father Cipriano Barace is killed while traveling among the Baures
1709	Conversion of the Baures begins with the founding of the Concepción Mission

1710	Expedition from Santa Cruz captures 2,000 Itonomas Indios and is condemned by the king
1715	Provincial Antonio Garriga visits the Mojos missions
1750	Spain and Portugal sign the *Tratado de Limites* to define the boundary between Brazil and Spanish America
1759	Jesuits expelled from Portugal
1764	Jesuits expelled from France
1767	Jesuits expelled from Spain, Naples, and America
1768	Colonel Aymerich executes the expulsion order and replaces the Jesuits with secular clergy
1768–72	Colonel Aymerich is governor of Mojos
1773–85	Crisis and civil and religious corruption in the governance of Mojos
1786–92	Reforming government of Lázaro de Ribera
1820	Archives for the Mojos region stored at the Colegio San Pedro are burned during the Canichanas revolt against Governor Velasco
1825	Bolivian independence
1842	Mojos Province becomes the Beni Department
1862	Beginning of Mojos migration to the Amazon forest of Brazil for rubber harvesting

GLOSSARY

adelantado	title given to the commander of a border region, oftentimes the leader of an expedition of exploration or conquest
adobe	a building material composed of mud bricks, often mixed with straw and dried
alcalde	municipal authority, president of the *cabildo*
anta	foraging mammal with a thick skin often used for making shields
arroba	unit of measure equal to 25 pounds or 11.5 kilograms
balsa	raft
bandeira	expedition organized for exploration and slave raiding by Portuguese and Brazilians
bandeirantes	members of a *bandeira*
barbacoa	Arawak term for a raised platform
bebedero	rectangular roofed space for ceremonies and community events

bibosi	ficus fiber used for weaving and braiding
cabildo	municipal council
cántaro	measure of volume equal to 16 liters
cerro	hill
chacra	cultivated field
chicha	alcoholic beverage produced by fermenting maize or yucca
cuartel	multi-family residence in the missions, divided into separate spaces for each family
cura	priest
descubrimiento	discovery or expedition of discovery
encomendero	Spanish feudal lord, holder of an *encomienda*, who receives tribute
encomienda	land and population assigned to an *encomendero*
engenho	mill for processing sugar cane
entrada	expedition for discovery, exploration, and conquest
estado	measure of length equal to 1.57 meters
estolica	a stick used to shoot darts, like a slingshot
extranamiento	expulsion of the Jesuits in 1767–8
fanega	measure of volume equal to 55.5 liters
fiscal	public official who serves as a judge
islas	slightly raised areas in the Llanos de Mojos that do not flood
legua	league, equal to 5.57 kilometers
maloca	expedition/slave raids carried out by the Brazilian Portuguese
operario	term used for the religious personnel of the missions
orejón	Spanish nickname for Incan nobles
parcialidad	a part of a village or community distinguished by family, clan, or ethnic links

peste	generic term for epidemics
pieza	or *pieza de Indias*, slave
planilla	prospect or table containing an annual assessment of the population of a mission
poblar	term used to describe the foundation of a Spanish village or settlement
quirquincho	armadillo
reducción	the action of "reducing" or concentrating outlying Indios in planned villages, often laid out on a gridwork model; synonymous with mission
regidores	adviser to the *cabildo*
rescates	normally these consist of tools or other instruments – hatchets, wedges, machetes, knives, needles, hooks – or adornments and baubles used as barter or gifts with the Indios
sabana	vast level areas without trees in the tropics
sarampión	measles
siringa	*Hevea brasiliensis*, the rubber tree
siringuero	worker employed in the gathering of rubber
soroche	illness caused by the lack of oxygen at high altitudes
surazos	cold winds coming from the south
tipoy	short cotton skirt
vara	measure of length equal to 83.6 centimeters
vecino	Spanish resident family or resident
viruela	smallpox
yanacona	servant in Spanish homes or farms
zapallo	vegetable from the squash family
zipa	*cacique*, head

APPENDIX

TAB. A.0 Population of the Missions, 1696–1831

Mission	Year of foundation	1691	1713	1720	1732	1736	1748	1797	1811	1831
1 Loreto	1682	3,822	2,923	1,624	1,235	1,150	1,054	1,697	1,411	2,014
2 Trinidad	1687	2,253	2,772	2,260	2,208	1,944	1,720	2,454	2,081	2,645
3 S. Francisco Xavier	1691	2,361	2,000	2,026	1,713	1,661	1,180			1,388
4 S. Pedro	1697		2,806	3,143	323	3,294	3,296	2,544		1,676
5 Exaltación de la Cruz	1709		1,401	1,842	1,851	1,915	1,593	1,156	1,376	2,073
6 S. Ana	1719			570	1,378	1,376	1,395	837	770	1,156
7 S. Rosa	1705, 1743		401	719	624	257				
8 Desposorios B.V.M.	1694, 1723		1,592	1,543	1,623	1,943	1,199			
9 S. José	1691	2,036	2,105	1,152	923	914	686			
10 S. Ignacio	1689	3,014	2,843	1,980	974	1,034	612	1,395		1,948
11 S. Luis Gonzaga	1698		1,628	1,358	906	747	523			
12 S. Francisco de Borja	1693	3,000	1,823	2,210	1,826	1,540	98			
13 S. Pablo	1703		1,380	2,199	2,020	1,520	1,225			
14 Los SS Reyes	1702, 1710		1,490	1,909	2,108	2,034	1,780	724		900
15 S. Joaquín	1709		1,204	2,810	2,632	2,833	2,121	554	734	690
16 S. Juan Bautista	1710		1,304	664						
17 Concepción B.V.M.	1708		2,817	2,578	3,151	3,277	2,803	2,229		3,033
18 S. María Magdalena	1720			1,208	2,782	2,861	3,112	3,191	3,965	2,669
19 S. Martín	1717			1,561	1,557	1,615	1,222			
20 S. Nicolas				1,203	1,514	2,048	1,816			
21 S. Miguel	1696, 1725				1,198	2,056	3,444			
22 Patrocinio B.V.M.	1730				909	1,325				
23 S. Simón	1744									
24 S. Ramón								3,564	3,858	1,893

TAB. A.0 Population of the Missions, 1696–1831 (continued)

Mission	Year of foundation	1691	1713	1720	1732	1736	1748	1797	1811	1831
25 Asunción B.V.M.				817						
26 Carmen										897
1–8 Totale Rio Mamoré		8,436	13,895	13,727	10,955	13,540	11,437	8,688		10,952
9–14 Totale Pampas		8,050	11,269	10,808	8,757	7,789	4,924	2,119		2,848
15–24 Totale Baures			5,325	10,024	13,743	16,015	14,518	9,538		8,285
25–26 Totale altre				817						897
1–26 TOTALE		16,846	30,489	35,376	33,455	37,344	30,879	20,345		22,982

Note: According to Barnadas, Santa Ana was abandoned for "*peste*" and joined with Loreto in 1740; the abandonment of San José (1752) and San Luis Gonzaga (1758) and also that of San Miguel were similarly imputed to "*peste*"; San Juan Bautista was instead abandoned in 1718 following attacks by the Guarayos, and Patrocinio B.V.M. in 1741 for apostasy. The data for 1811, taken from Moreno, are incomplete. See Barnadas, "Introducción," in Eder, *Breve descripción*; Moreno, *Catálogo*.

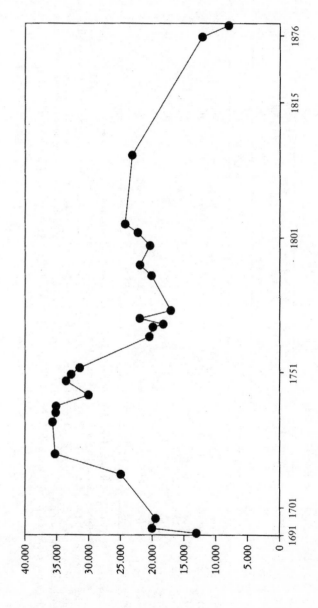

Fig. A.1.   Population of the Mojos, 1691–1876.

TAB. A.1 Demographic indices, 1713–1831

	Children	Married	Total	Children per married woman or couple	Children per 100 inhabitants	Married per 100 inhabitants	Persons per family
	VALORI ASSOLUTI			RAPORTI			
1713	14,518	4,742	23,389	6.12	62.1	20.3	9.86
1720	9,830	14,586	28,819	1.35	34.1	50.6	3.95
1732	11,070	18,799	36,445	1.18	30.4	51.6	3.88
1736	11,713	16,511	33,283	1.42	35.2	49.6	4.03
1748	11,957	15,221	31,779	1.57	37.6	47.9	4.18
1752	12,282	15,376	30,685	1.60	40.0	50.1	3.99
1764	8,446	10,958	21,793	1.54	38.8	50.3	3.98
1831	10,500	11,416	22,883	1.84	45.9	49.9	4.01

Sources: For 1713: Pablo Pastells, *Historia de la Compañía de Jesús en la Provincia de Paraguay*, 8 vols. (vols. VI–VII with Francisco Mateos), Madrid: Victoriano Suárez, 1912–49, vol. IV, frontispeice. For 1720: Catalogus Missionum, ARSI, Perú, 7, f. 62. For 1732: Catalogus Reductionum, ARSI, Perú, 7, f. 89. For 1736: Catalogus Reductionum, ARSI, Perú, 7, ff. 65 and 65v. For 1748: Catálogo de las Misiones, Pastells, *Historia*, vol. VII, pp. 746–8. For 1752: Block, *In Search of El Dorado*, p. 299; «El Gobernado», AGI, Charcas, 474, ff. 4v.–6. For 1764: Catálogo y Numeración, in Manuel A. Fuentes, *Memorias de los Virreyes que han gobernado el Perú durante el tiempo colonial español*, 6 vols., Lima: Librería Central Felipe Baily, 1859, vol. IV, pp. 4–5. For 1831: D'Orbigny, *Descripción geográfica*, p. 331.

TAB. A.2 Demographic indices by district, 1732, 1736 and 1748

District	Children per		Married men per		Unmarried men per 100 adult males	Unmarried women per 100 adult females	Widowed per 100 married	Male children per 100 female children	Men per 100 women	Persons per family
	married woman	100 inhabitants	100 adult males	family or couple						
1732										
Rio Mamoré	1.09	28.7	70.9	76.2	18.4	12.5	7.8	114.2	109.3	3.82
Pampas	1.31	33.4	74.5	79.1	14.5	10.6	7.1	124.2	111.9	3.92
Baure	1.18	30.2	71.4	74.9	19.5	15.3	6.6	116.8	108.3	3.92
TOTAL	1.18	30.4	71.9	76.4	17.9	13.1	7.2	117.7	109.5	3.88
1736										
Rio Mamoré	1.44	35.5	74.4	77.7	18.8	13.7	5.0	103.0	103.9	4.07
Pampas	1.39	35.8	77.2	83.5	14.6	9.7	4.8	104.3	106.8	3.88
Baures	1.41	27.0	72.5	77.5	20.0	14.5	3.9	113.3	109.1	5.24
TOTAL	1.42	31.8	74.3	78.9	18.3	13.1	4.5	107.0	106.4	4.46
1748										
Rio Mamoré	1.61	36.1	80.5	80.7	11.7	10.2	4.7	104.4	101.9	4.46
Pampas	1.15	33.4	91.7	90.3	5.8	5.2	2.3	112.2	103.0	3.44
Baures	1.77	38.0	75.2	82.0	18.1	8.3	4.5	122.0	114.2	4.66
TOTAL	1.57	36.5	80.4	83.2	13.3	8.4	4.2	113.5	107.3	4.31
Average for the 3 years										
Rio Mamoré	1.38	33.4	75.3	78.2	16.3	12.1	5.8	107.2	105.0	4.11
Pampas	1.28	34.2	81.1	84.3	11.6	8.5	4.7	113.6	107.2	3.75
Baures	1.45	31.7	73.1	78.2	19.2	12.7	5.0	117.4	110.5	4.61
TOTAL	1.39	32.9	75.6	79.5	16.5	11.5	5.3	112.7	107.8	4.22

Source: See Table A.1.

TAB. A.3 Fertility and mortality in the Llanos, 1828–31

	Births			Deaths			Population
	male	female	Total	male	female	Total	
1828	767	805	1,572	590	500	1,090	22,381
1829	807	733	1,540	574	505	1,075	22,846
1830	807	784	1,591	562	560	1,122	23,315
1831	695	690	1,385	–	–	2,798	22,883

	Male births per 100 female births	Fertility (per 1,000)	Male deaths per 100 female deaths	Mortality (per 1,000)	Population increase (per 1,000)
1828	95.28	70.24	118.00	48.70	21.54
1829	110.10	67.41	113.66	47.05	20.35
1830	102.93	68.24	100.36	48.12	20.12
1831	100.72	60.53	–	122.27	-61.75

Source: D'Orbigny, *Descripción geográfica*, pp. 336–42.

SOURCES FOR ILLUSTRATIONS

Life in the missions

These illustrations (Plates 10–34) were made by the Jesuit Florian Pauke (Witzingen 1729–Neuhaus 1780), who was in America from 1749 to 1768 and directed the mission of San Javier among the Macobies Indios of Chacos (in the present-day province of Santa Fe in Argentina). The collective scenes, flora, and fauna are analogous to those of the Mojos. Pauke returned to Austria after the expulsion of the Jesuits from America and, like other members of his Order, recorded his missionary experiences in a manuscript, kept today in the Abbey of Zwittl and complemented by a rich collection of watercolors. These reproductions are taken from the complete edition published in Spanish: Florian Pauke, *Hacia allá y para acá (una estada entre los indios Macobies, 1749–1767)*, Tacumán-Buenos Aires: Universidad Nacional de Tacumán, 3 vols., 1942–4 (translation by Edmundo Wernicke).

Maps by Vander and Lastarria

The first (Map 3) comes from the mid-sixteenth century and the second (Map 10) from the last third of the eighteenth century. They are taken from *Exposición de la República del Perú presentado al Ecxmo Gobierno Argentino en el Juicio de Límites con la República de Bolivia*, 2 vols., Barcelona: Imprenta Heinrich, 1906, vol. I.

Eighteenth-century map of the Llanos

This map (Map 8) is taken from Guillermo Furlong, *Cartografía jesuítica del Río de la Plata*, 2 vols., Buenos Aires: Jacobo Peuser, 1936; it is the fifteenth map of volume II and, according to Furlong, is the work of the Creole Father Javier Iraizos, born in Cochabamba around 1756 (see pp. 86–7 of vol. I). The map is strangely rotated 90 degrees: the Guapay-Mamoré river flows south to north and not east to west as shown in the map.

Gold objects

Plates 1–9 depict gold objects kept in the Museo del Oro del Banco de la República, Bogotá.

NOTES AND REFERENCES

Chapter I

1 Bartolomé de Las Casas, *Historia de las Indias*, 3 vols., México: Fondo de Cultura Económica, II ed., 1995, vol. II, p. 216.

2 Gonzalo Fernández de Oviedo, *Historia General y Natural de las Indias*, 5 vols., Madrid: Atlas, 1992, vol. I, p. 70.

3 Las Casas, *Historia*, vol. II, pp. 225–6.

4 Pietro Martire d'Anghiera, *Mondo nuovo*, Milan: Alpes, 1930, p. 368.

5 Earl Hamilton, *American Treasure and the Price Revolution in Spain 1501–1650*, Cambridge, Mass.: Harvard University Press, 1934, tab. 3. On gold production in Hispaniola, see also Massimo Livi Bacci, "Return to Hispaniola. Reassessing a Demographic Catastrophe," *The Hispanic American Historical Review*, LXXXIII, 2003, n.1, tab. 3, p. 16.

6 Oviedo, *Historia*, vol. V, p. 62 includes the report of Francisco de Xerés. For a modern version, see Francisco

de Xerés, *Verdadera relación del Perú*. Madrid: Biblioteca de Autores Españoles, vol. XXVI, 1947, pp. 320–46. For the English version cited here, see Clements R. Markham, ed., *Reports on the Discovery of Peru*, London: Hakluyt Society, 1872, p. 65. See also Frederick A. Kirkpatrick, *The Spanish Conquistadores*, London: A&C Black, 1934, pp. 161–2.

7 Oviedo, *Historia*, vol. V, pp. 79–80.

8 For a complete history of Pizarro's men as well as the division of the treasure, see James Lockhart, *The Men of Cajamarca: A Social and Biographical Study of the First Conquerors of Peru*, Austin: University of Texas Press, 1972.

9 A *fanega* is equivalent to 58 liters.

10 Francisco de Xeres in Markham, ed., *Reports on the Discovery of Peru*, pp. 108–9. See also Oviedo, *Historia*, vol. V, p. 165; Kirkpatrick, *The Spanish Conquistadores*, pp. 163–5.

11 Lockhart, *Men of Cajamarca*, pp. 78–80.

12 Ibid., pp. 96–7.

13 Oviedo, *Historia*, vol. V, p. 81.

14 John Hemming, *The Conquest of the Incas*, New York: Harcourt, Brace, Jovanovich, 1970, pp. 131–2.

15 Lockhart, *Men of Cajamarca*, pp. 44–6.

16 Constantino Bayle, *El Dorado fantasma*, Madrid: Publicaciones del Consejo de la Hispanidad, 1943, pp. 201–3.

17 Juan Rodríguez Freyle, *Conquista y descubrimiento del Nuevo Reyno de Granada*, Madrid: Dastin Historia, 2000. Manuel Lucena Salmoral, *Ximénez de Quesada, el caballero de El Dorado*, Madrid: Anaya, 1988.

18 Oviedo, *Historia*, vol. III, p. 124; Lucena Salmoral, *Ximénez de Quesada*, pp. 46–7.

19 Pedro Cieza de León, *La crónica del Perú*, Madrid: Historia 16, 1984, pp. 387–8.

20 Already in 1538, Diego de Almagro together with the survivors of the failed expedition to Chile had confronted the followers of Pizarro led by Hernando near Cuzco; Almagro was beaten in the Battle of Las Salinas. That conflict began a long season of devastating and bloody civil wars that only came to a definitive end in 1554.

21 Hamilton, *American Treasure*, p. 42. According to Hamilton's calculations, the gold imported to Seville by decade amounted to 4,965 kilograms (1503–10); 9,153 kilograms (1511–20); 4,889 kilograms (1521–30); 14,466 kilograms (1531–40); 24,957 kilograms (1541–50); 42,630 kilograms (1551–60); and 11,531 kilograms (1561–70).

22 Bayle, *El Dorado*, p. 25.

23 "Derecho de escobilla," literally "the right of the broom" or the rich privilege granted by the king to collect the gold shavings and residue in those places where gold was cast or coins minted.

24 Oviedo, *Historia*, vol. V, p. 236; the story was told again a century later in Freyle, *Conquista y descubrimiento*, pp. 63–4.

25 Bayle, *El Dorado*, p. 26.

26 Oviedo, *Historia*, vol. II, p. 102.

27 Oviedo, *Historia*, vol. III, p. 42.

28 Alexander von Humboldt and Aimé Bonpland, *Personal Narrative of Travels to the Equinoctial Regions of the New Continent, during the Years 1799–1804*, London: Longman, 1821. Notes on the location of El Dorado are spread throughout the work, but are summarized in vol. V, pt. 2, pp. 773–864 in an exposition that Humboldt would contribute in 1841 to a book of travel writings on Guyana and the Orinoco.

29 Bayle, *El Dorado*, pp. 204–10.

30 Oviedo, *Historia*, vol. III, p. 99.

31 Bayle, *El Dorado*, pp. 218–21.
32 Kirkpatrick, *The Spanish Conquistadores*, pp. 304–9; Bayle, *El Dorado*, p. 118.
33 Bayle, *El Dorado*, pp. 119–26.
34 Humboldt and Bonpland, *Personal Narrative*, vol. V, pt. 2, pp. 820–23.
35 Kirkpatrick, *The Spanish Conquistadores*, pp. 229–37.
36 Ibid.
37 Gaspar de Carvajal, *Relación que escribió Fr. Gaspar de Carvajal, fraile de la orden de Santo Domingo de Guzman, del nuevo descubrimiento del famoso río grande que descubrió por muy gran ventura el Capitán Francisco de Orellana*, in Aa.Vv., *La aventura del Amazonas*, Madrid: Historia 16, 1986. For an English translation, see José Toribio Medina, ed., *The Discovery of the Amazon according to the Account of Friar Gaspar de Carvajal and other Documents*, New York: American Geographical Society, 1934.
38 Las Casas, *Historia*, vol. I, pp. 303–4.
39 Medina, ed., *The Discovery of the Amazon*, p. 214.
40 Ibid., pp. 219–22.
41 Oviedo, *Historia*, vol. V, p. 242.
42 Ibid., vol. V, p. 197. According to Herrera, there were 1,600 Spanish soldiers at Cuzco, armed, poorly disciplined, and all ready for adventure (Antonio de Herrera, *Historia general de los hechos de los castellanos en las isles y tierrafirme del mar Océano (1601–1615)*, 10 vols., Asunción: Editorial Guarania, 1946–47, vol. VII, p. 338.
43 Bayle, *El Dorado*, p. 251.
44 According to the testimony of Augustín de Zárate, cited in Kirkpatrick, *The Spanish Conquistadores*, p. 208.
45 Lockhart, *Men of Cajamarca*, pp. 129–33.
46 Herrera, *Historia general*, vol. VII, pp. 338–40.
47 Ibid., p. 341.
48 Kirkpatrick, *The Spanish Conquistadores*, p. 206.

49 Roberto Levillier, *El Paititi, el Dorado y las Amazonas*, Buenos Aires: Emecé Editores, 1976.

50 Kirkpatrick, *The Spanish Conquistadores*, p. 207.

51 Levillier, *El Paititi*, p. 101.

52 Ibid., p. 102.

53 José Chávez Suárez, *Historia de Moxos*, La Paz: Editorial Don Bosco, 1986, p. 59.

54 Cieza de León, *La crónica del Perú*, p. 386.

55 Levillier, *El Paititi*, pp. 42–5; Enrique Finot, *Historia de la Conquista del Oriente Boliviano*, La Paz: Editorial Juventud, 1978, pp. 147–8.

56 Domingo de Santo Tomás, "Lettera al Consiglio delle Indie del 1° Luglio 1550," cited in Rubén Vargas Ugarte, *Historia general del Perú*. II: *Virreinato 1550–1600*, Lima: C. Milla Batres, 1966, p. 37.

Chapter II

1 On the geography, nature, and culture of the Llanos, see William M. Denevan's classic study, *The Aboriginal Cultural Geography of the Llanos de Mojos in Bolivia*, Berkeley-Los Angeles: University of California Press, 1966. Another work that deals at length with this topic and others is David Block, "In Search of El Dorado: Spanish Entry into Moxos, A Tropical Frontier, 1550–1767," PhD diss., Austin: University of Texas at Austin, 1980.

2 Leandro Tormo Sanz, "Historia demográfica de las Misiones de Mojos," *Missionalia Hispanica*, XXXV–XXXVI, 1978, pp. 291–2.

3 As we shall describe below, the area of the Llanos covers about 180,000 square kilometers and makes up much of the Department of Beni, itself covering 214,000 kilometers (about one-fifth the area of Bolivia) and numbering 411,000 inhabitants in 2005 (4.5 percent of the national

population) with a density of barely 1.9 people per square kilometer. Around the middle of the nineteenth century, that density was 0.7. These numbers should be kept in mind when we consider demographic estimates for the seventeenth century that suggest a higher density than that of the present day.

4 Denevan, *The Aboriginal*, p. 5.

5 Diego Francisco Altamirano, *Historia de la Mision de los Mojos*, La Paz: IBC, 1979, p. 45. Altamirano was Jesuit superior of the province and both visited the Llanos and took part in evangelical work among the Baures. He is one of the principal sources of information about the society and native culture of the region between the late seventeenth century and the beginning of the eighteenth century. He wrote his history between 1703 and 1715, but had already written in 1699 a *Breve noticia de las Misiones de Moxos* in which he deals with many of the topics included in the larger work cited above.

6 Alcides D'Orbigny, *Descripción geográfica, histórica y estadística de Bolivia*, Paris: Librairie Gide, 1845, p. 357.

7 "Carta del Padre Antonio de Orellana sobre el origen de las misiones de los Mojos (18 de Octubre de 1687)," in Victor Maurtua, ed., *Juicio de límites entre Perú y Bolivia*, Imp. de Gabriel L. y de Horno, 1906, vol. X, p. 8.

8 Ibid., p. 18.

9 Altamirano, *Historia*, p. 39.

10 D'Orbigny, *Descripción geográfica*, p. 356.

11 Ibid., p. 245.

12 Leandro Tormo Sanz, ed., "El padre Julian de Aller y su relación de Mojos," *Missionalia Hispanica*, XIII, 1956, p. 377.

13 Gabriel René Moreno, *Catálogo del Archivo de Mojos y Chiquitos*, La Paz: Librería Editorial Juventud, 1974, p. 52.

14 "Carta del Padre Antonio de Orellana," in Maurtua, ed., *Juicio de límites*, vol. X, pp. 18–19.

15 Denevan, *The Aboriginal*, p. 18.

16 Ibid.; Moreno, *Catálogo*, p. 14.

17 Denevan, *The Aboriginal*, p. 43.

18 José del Castillo, "Relación de la provincia de Mojos," in Manuel V. Ballivián, *Documentos para la historia geográfica de la República de Bolivia*, La Paz: Gamarra, 1906, pp. 294–302. This is a transcription of Brother José del Castillo's original, which can be found in the Archivo Nacional del Perú.

19 Joseph M. Barnadas, "Introducción," in Francisco J. Eder, *Breve descripción de las reducciones de los Mojos*, Cochabamba: Historia Boliviana, 1985, p. XXXIII. Barnadas's study is the most complete history available of the Mojos during the Jesuit period. For a shortened version, see idem, "Las reducciones Jesuíticas de Mojos," *Historia Boliviana*, IV, 1984, n. 2.

20 Moreno, *Catálogo*, p. 46.

21 Ibid., p. 15.

22 Altamirano, *Historia*, p. 52.

23 Del Castillo, "Relación de la provincia de Mojos," in Ballivián, *Documentos*, p. 310.

24 Ibid., pp. 319–20.

25 Horacio A. Calandra and Susana A. Salceda, "Amazonia boliviana. Arqueología de los Llanos de Mojos," *Acta Amazonica*, XXXIV, 2004, n. 2.

26 Altamirano, *Historia*, p. 123.

27 Block, *In Search of El Dorado*, p. 73.

28 Altamirano, *Historia*, p. 120; del Castillo, "Relación de la provincia de Mojos," in Ballivián, *Documentos*, p. 341.

29 Altamirano, *Historia*, p. 53.

30 Del Castillo, "Relación de la provincia de Mojos," in Ballivián, *Documentos*, p. 30.

31 Block, *In Search of El Dorado*, p. 57.
32 Del Castillo, "Relación de la provincia de Mojos," in Ballivián, *Documentos*, p. 318.
33 Denevan, *The Aboriginal*, pp. 74–83; Clark L. Erikson, "Archaeological Methods for the Study of Ancient Landscapes of the Llanos de Mojos in the Bolivian Amazon," in Peter Stahl, ed., *Archaeology in the Lowland American Tropics. Current Analytical Methods and Applications*. Cambridge: Cambridge University Press, 1995.
34 Altamirano, *Historia*, pp. 50–1; del Castillo, "Relación de la provincia de Mojos," in Ballivián, *Documentos*, p. 319.
35 Del Castillo, "Relación de la provincia de Mojos," in Ballivián, *Documentos*, p. 308.
36 Altamirano, *Historia*, p. 118.
37 Ibid., p. 52.
38 Denevan, *The Aboriginal*, pp. 117 seq.; idem, "The Aboriginal Population of Amazonia," in William M. Denevan, ed., *The Native Population of the Americas in 1492*, Madison: University of Wisconsin Press, 1992, pp. 210–13.
39 Beginning in the 1960s, population estimates for pre-contact America – which authors in the first half of the century like Alfred Kroeber, Julian H. Steward, and Angel Rosenblat had put at relatively modest levels (between 8 and 15 million) – rapidly increased, reaching the figure of 113 million proposed by Henry Dobyns. This revision, which established a distinction between "high counters" and "low counters," was strongly influenced by the idea that indigenous populations, lacking resistance or immunization to Eurasian diseases, suffered a sustained and dramatic decline immediately following contact. Its major champions include Sherburne F. Cook, Woodrow Borah, and Henry Dobyns. On this topic, see Massimo Livi Bacci, *Conquest: The Destruction of the America Indios*, Cambridge: Polity, 2008.

40 Francisco Mateos, ed., *Historia general de la Compañía de Jesús en la Provincia del Perú*. II: *Relaciones de Colegios y Misiones*, Madrid: Consejo Superior de Investigaciones Sociales – Instituto Gonzalo Fernández de Oviedo, 1944. This work includes the "Crónica anónima" of 1600, the original of which is kept at ARSI, Peruana.

41 Altamirano, *Historia*, p. 47.

42 "Consultas hechas a S.M. por don Juan de Lizarazu, presidente de Charcas, sobre su entrada a los Moxos o Toros, años 1636–38," in Maurtua, ed., *Juicio de límites*, vol. IX, pp. 121–216. This "consultation" includes a transcription of the investigation ordered by the president of the Audiencia de Charcas on the exploration of the land of Mojos and the testimony of the surviviors of the expedition led by Gonzalo de Solís de Holguín in 1617.

43 Ibid., pp. 145–50.

44 Ibid., p. 158.

45 Ibid., p. 169.

46 Ibid., p. 165.

47 Ibid., p. 169.

48 A *fanega* could hold approximately 25 kilograms of ears of maize. The amount of food in each depositary was "'twenty or thirty *fanegas*,'" here taken as 25 on average; the observers "counted" 1,200 depositaries. We have calculated then that each person needs 300 kilograms of maize per year and that the quantity of food available in ears ($25 \times 25 \times 1200 = 750,000\,\text{kg}$) should be divided by two in order to obtain the amount consumable: $750,000 \div 2 \div 300 = 1,250$ people. Here too we are dealing with a hypothetical exercise aimed at obtaining an order of magnitude for the sake of comparison.

49 "Consultas hechas," in Maurtua, ed., *Juicio de límites*, vol. IX, pp. 187–97.

50 Del Castillo, "Relación de la provincia de Mojos," in Ballivián, *Documentos.*

51 José del Castillo's observations can be summed up as follows: he found forty-one villages, but for nine of these did not specify population size. Of the other thirty-two, two had an average population of 175; ten of 55; eight of 62; five of 60; six of 58; and one of 70. On average, the population of these thirty-two villages was, according to the Jesuit, 66 people or 10–15 families.

52 Leandro Tormo Sanz, "Situación y población de los Mojos en 1679," *Revista Española de Antropologia Americana*, VII, 1972, n. 2. Tormo Sanz transcribed some of the "Relación de los P.P. de la Misión de los Infideles Mojos" of 12 July, 1679, signed by Fathers Marbán, Barace, and Ygarza; the original is in ARSI, Perú, 20, ff. 228–30.

53 Block, *In Search of El Dorado*, p. 52.

54 Altamirano, *Historia*, p. 132.

55 Ibid., p. 30.

56 Diego de Eguiluz, *Relación de la Misión Apostólica de los Mojos, escrita en 1696*, Lima: Imprenta del Universo, 1884. Eguiluz was the provincial Father of Perú before Altamirano, and much of his *Relación* is based on the *Carta del Padre Antonio de Orellana* of 1687, cited above.

57 Altamirano, *Historia*, pp. 132–3.

58 Ibid., p. 164.

59 Eguiluz, *Relación*, p. 35.

60 Altamirano, *Historia*, p. 110; Barnadas, "Introducción," in Eder, *Breve descripción*, p. XXXVII.

Chapter III

1 "'Consultas hechas,'" in Maurtua, ed., *Juicio de límites*, vol. IX, p. 155.

2 Ibid., p. 121.

3 Ibid.

4 Bayle, *El Dorado*, p. 240.

5 Juan de Betanzos, witness to the first phase of the Conquest, also referred to Incan expansion across the Andes. See Juan de Betanzos, *Suma y narración de los Incas*, Madrid: Ediciones Poliremo, 2004, p. 370.

6 Garcilaso de la Vega, *Royal Commentaries of the Incas, and General History of Peru*, Austin: University of Texas Press, p. 434–5. The Amarumayu would seem to be the Madre de Dios.

7 Ibid., pp. 436–7.

8 Ibid., p. 438.

9 Levillier, *El Paititi*.

10 Ibid., pp. 97–9; *Exposición de la República del Perú presentada al Ecxmo Gobierno Argentino en el Juicio de Límites con la República de Bolivia*, 2 vols., Barcelona: Imprenta Heinrich, 1906, vol. I, p. 17.

11 *Exposición de la República del Perú*, vol. I, p. 249.

12 Chávez Suárez, *Historia de Moxos*, p. 59.

13 "Real Cédula de SM ordinando no se dén a persona alguna el descubrimiento de los Moxos, 23 agosto de 1573," in Maurtua, ed., *Juicio de límites*, vol. IX, pp. 74–81.

14 Ibid., p. 74.

15 "Relación de los descubrimientos o pretendidos y realizados a oriente de la cordillera de los Andes – Año 1570," in Maurtua, ed., *Juicio de límites*, vol. IX, pp. 37–42.

16 The exploits of Maldonado are well described in Levillier, *El Paititi*, pp. 103–12, of which I have made liberal use. See also *Exposición de la República del Perú*, vol. I; Bayle, *El Dorado*, pp. 255–6.

17 De la Vega, *Royal Commentaries*, pp. 441–2.

18 Bayle, *El Dorado*, p. 241.

19 Levillier, *El Paititi*, p. 112.

20 Juan López de Velasco, *Geografía y descripción universal de las Indias*, Madrid: Atlas, 1971, pp. 282–3.

21 Levillier, *El Paititi*, p. 225; Finot, *Historia de la Conquista*, pp. 90–2.

22 Finot, *Historia de la Conquista*, pp. 85–6.

23 Levillier, *El Paititi*, p. 227; The great voyager Félix de Azara wrote: "The famous Xarayes Lake is formed by the flowing together of all the water produced by the abundant rains that fall during the months of November, December, January, and February in the Chiquitos province and in all the mountains whose run-off contributes to make the great Paraguay River." Cited in Finot, *Historia de la Conquista*, p. 35.

24 Ibid., pp. 160–1. Levillier disagrees regarding the itinerary of Chaves.

25 Ibid.

26 "Descripción geográfica y estadística de la Provincia de Santa Cruz de la Sierra, de Don Francisco de Viedma, su Gobernador-Intendente," in *Collecíon de obras y documentos de las Provincias del Río de la Plata, illustradas con notas y disertaciones por Pedro de Angelis*, vol. III, Buenos Aires, 1886.

27 "Crónica anónima del 1600 que trata del establecimiento y misiones de la Compañía de Jesús en los paises de habla española en la América meridional," ARSI, Perú, 23, f. 441. See also Mateos, ed., *Historia general*, vol. II.

28 "Crónica anónima," f. 446.

29 Block, *In Search of El Dorado*, p. 175.

30 Finot, *Historia de la Conquista*, pp. 266–9; Block, *In Search of El Dorado*, pp. 166–8.

31 Tormo Sanz, "Historia demográfica," p. 295.

32 "Crónica anónima," f. 445.

33 Finot, *Historia de la Conquista*, p. 274.

34 "Relación de lo sucedido en la jornada de los Mojos año de 1667," ARSI, Perú, 20, ff. 130–38v.

35 Ibid., f. 130v.

36 Ibid., f. 131v.

37 Ibid., f. 137.

38 Ibid., ff. 137 and 137v.

39 "Crónica anónima," f. 443.

40 Ibid.

41 "Real Cédula para que la audiencia de Charcas proceda al castigo del Gobernador y vecinos de Santa Cruz de la Sierra por su entrada a los indios Ytonomas," in Maurtua, ed., *Juicio de límites*, vol. X, p. 44.

Chapter IV

1 Francisco Mateos, "Avances portugueses y misiones españolas en la América del Sur," *Missionalia Hispánica*, 1948, n.15, pp. 462–3 and 1–24.

2 Ibid., pp. 461–2.

3 Rubén Vargas Ugarte, *Historia de la iglesia en el Perú*. II: *1570–1640*, Burgos: Imprenta de Aldecoa, 1959, p. 250.

4 Lazaro de Aspurz, "Magnitud del esfuerzo misionero de España," *Missionalia Hispánica*, III, 1946, n. 7; Antonio Astrain, *Historia de la Campañía de Jesús en la Asistencia de España*. IV: *1581–1615*, Madrid: Razón y Fe, 1913.

5 Sabina Pavone, *I gesuiti*, Rome-Bari: Laterza, 2004. Pavone maintains that "the missions outside of Europe were often used as places to send individuals who had become embarrassing from a political or religious point of view... or else simply a psychological one. This last point would seem to be confirmed by the catalog from a province like Brazil which reveals a large number of Fathers suffering from notable character defects (*collericus* is the recurring adjective)" (pp. 67–8). In Santa Cruz too there were many Jesuits whose character was *collericus*. And it is perhaps not surprising that the people more likely to go to difficult areas requiring new conversions

be more sanguine, perhaps less inclined to teaching and study but better versed in practical things and able to organize matters on the ground, to offer instruction in the "mechanical arts," and in agriculture and medicine. There were, for example, many individuals of this sort on the Paraguay missions. Indeed it would be worthwhile to evaluate the specific abilities of the individual missionaries in order to test the statement that "those who were chosen for distant postings tended not to be the most sound individuals" (Ibid., p. 67).

6 Geronimo Pallas, "Missión a las Indias, con advertencias para los Religiosos de Europa que la huvieron de emprender como primero se verá en la historia de un viaje y después en discurso" [Lima, 1620], ff. 433. The manuscript can be found at ARSI, Perú, 23; the quotation can be found in f. 291.

7 Ibid.

8 José María García Recio, "La Iglesia en Santa Cruz de la Sierra (Bolivia). 1560–1606," *Missionalia Hispánica*, 1983, n. 118.

9 "Relación de la Misión de los Mojos" (to the R.P. Provincial, Juan de Soto, 3 November, 1668), ARSI, Perú, 20, ff. 142–4v and 148–9b v.

10 Ibid., f. 143.

11 Tormo Sanz, ed., "El padre Julian de Aller," p. 375. The text transcribed by Tormo Sanz, "Relación que el padre Julián de Aller," is kept in the Biblioteca de la Academia de la Historia, Colección Jesuitas, vol. XII, f. 20.

12 Ibid., p. 375.

13 Though Father Marbán, who as we shall see later compiled and published a grammar of the Mojo language, claimed that the work of Father Áller was not much help, based as it was on only a few days spent among the Mojos.

14 "Carta del Padre Antonio de Orellana," in Maurtua, ed., *Juicio de límites*, vol. X, p. 3. The "Carta del Padre Antonio de Orellana" is transcribed almost letter for letter in the first part of Diego de Eguiluz's chronicle (see n. 24) and by other subsequent chroniclers. Those chronicles together with the letters and reports held in ARSI constitute the most direct and reliable source for the early missionary period.

15 "Istrucción que dió el Padre Hernando Cabero, Vice Provincial y Visitador de esta provinicia a los PP. Pedro Marbán y Cipriano Baraze y al H.no Joseph del Castillo que fueron a explorar la Misión de los Mojos infieles," ARSI, Perú, 20, ff. 166–7.

16 Ibid., ff. 166 and 166v.

17 "Carta de los PP que residen en la misión de los Moxos para el P Hernando Cavero de la Compañía de J. Provincial de esta provincia del Perú en que le se da la noticia de lo que han visto oído en el tiempo que han estado en ella (20 abril de 1676)," ARSI, Perú, 20, ff. 200–13.

18 "Copia de la Relación del Padre Cipriano Barace sobre la conversión de los Indios infieles," in reply to a letter from the provincial of 30 November, 1679. This letter is cataloged as 17 September, 1680, but was written on 6 May, 1680. ARSI, Perú, 20, ff. 232–237v.

19 "Ordenes y información que hiço el P. Cavero provincial desta provincia con los pareceres de los P.P. O.O. para los padres de la Misión de los Mojos, 8 deciembre 1676," ARSI, Perú, 20, ff. 214–214v.

20 "Carta del Padre Antonio de Orellana," in Maurtua, ed., *Juicio de límites*, vol. X, p. 14.

21 "Copia de la Relación del Padre Cipriano Barace," ff. 233v–234v.

22 "Carta del Padre Antonio de Orellana," in Maurtua, ed., *Juicio de límites*, vol. X, p. 15–16.

23 Ibid., p. 16.

24 Eguiluz, *Relación*. Using letters from the missionaries and, for the events up to 1687, copying almost word for word the "Carta del Padre Antonio de Orellana," Eguiluz, the Jesuit provincial, provides detailed information on the founding of the first six missions.

25 See note 24.

26 Eguiluz, *Relación*, p. 62.

27 Ibid.

28 Eguiluz's population figures were taken from the *padrón* (count) made in August 1691 during a visit from the governor of Santa Cruz de la Sierra, Benito de Rivera Quiroga, and updates supplied by the Fathers.

29 Eguiluz, *Relación*, pp. 17–18.

30 Ibid., pp. 26, 28.

31 Antonio Astrain, *Historia de la Compañía de Jesús en la Asistencia de España*. VI: *1652–1705*, Madrid: Razón y Fe, 1920, pp. 556–7.

32 Block, *In Search of El Dorado*, pp. 208–9.

33 Altamirano, *Historia*; chapters XIV and XV include the narrative synthesized here. See also Astrain, *Historia de la Compañía*, pp. 565 seq.

34 Altamirano, *Historia*, ch. XIV.

35 Astrain, *Historia de la Compañía*, pp. 570–1.

36 Altamirano, *Historia*, p. 106.

37 Ibid.

38 Ibid., p. 107

39 Ibid., pp. 109–15.

40 "Relación de las Misiones de los Mojos de la Comp. Jhs en la Prov.a del Peru el año 1713," ARSI, Perú, 21, f. 179.

41 On the Paraguay missions, see Livi Bacci, *Conquest*, ch. VIII.

Chapter V

1 Denevan, *The Native Population*, pp. XVIII and 3; 113 million is Dobyns' "maximum" estimate (his minimum is 90 million).

2 Those testimonies gave rise to the so-called *Leyenda Negra* regarding the cruel nature of the Conquest, especially in its early phase before the Spanish administration imposed a degree of law and order. The small volume that Las Casas published in Seville in 1552 (Bartolomé de Las Casas, *Brevísima relación de la destruición de las Indias*, Madrid: Cátedra, 1996 [English translation: Bartolomé de Las Casas, *A Short Account of the Destruction of the Indies*, London: Penguin Books, 1992]) supplied explosive fuel for the *Leyenda*, subsequently used for both anti-Spanish and anti-Catholic purposes. In any case, most of the direct testimony attributes the demographic, social, and political disaster suffered by the Indios to multiple causes and not to the simple action of disease. For more on this interpretation, see Livi Bacci, *Conquest*, especially chapter 2.

3 Livi Bacci, *Conquest*, tables 2 and 3.

4 For a guide to these sources, see Barnadas, "Introducción," in Eder, *Breve descripción*.

5 The opening sections of both Eguiluz and Altamirano regarding the arrival of the Fathers among the Mojos are taken straight from the *Carta del Padre Antonio de Orellana*, cited above, of 1687.

6 José María Blanco, *Historia documentada de la vida y gloriosa muerte de los Padres Roque González de la Cruz, Alonso Rodríguez y Juan del Castillo de la Compañía de Jesús*, Buenos Aires: Mártires del Caaró y Yjuhi, 1929, p. 108.

7 D'Orbigny, *Descripción geográfica*, p. 379.

8 "Carta del Padre Antonio de Orellana," in Maurtua, ed., *Juicio de límites*, vol. X. p. 11.

9 Altamirano, *Historia*, p. 128.
10 Eder, *Breve descripción*, p. 282.
11 Ibid., p. 281.
12 Altamirano, *Historia*, pp. 127–8.
13 Ibid., p. 123.
14 Eder, *Breve descripción*, pp. 279–80.
15 Tormo Sanz, "El padre Julian de Aller," p. 380.
16 Eguiluz, *Relación*, p. 11.
17 Altamirano, *Historia*, p. 51.
18 Ibid.
19 Ibid., p. 52.
20 D'Orbigny, *Descripción geográfica*, p. 331.
21 "Carta del Padre Antonio de Orellana," in Maurtua, ed., *Juicio de límites*, vol. X. p. 17.
22 Eder, *Breve descripción*, p. 341.
23 "Carta del Padre Antonio de Orellana," in Maurtua, ed., *Juicio de límites*, vol. X. p. 12.
24 Altamirano, *Historia*, p. 35; D'Orbigny, *Descripción geográfica*, p. 188.
25 Altamirano, *Historia*, p. 35.
26 Eder, *Breve descripción*, p. 345.
27 Tormo Sanz, "El padre Julian de Aller," p. 380.
28 Eder, *Breve descripción*, p. 344.
29 D'Orbigny, *Descripción geográfica*, p. 336.
30 Eder, *Breve descripción*, p. 341.
31 Livi Bacci, *Conquest*, table 20.
32 Eder, *Breve descripción*, pp. 335–6; for the quotation from Father Messia, see "Relación de las Misiones de los Mojos de la Comp. Jhs en la Prov.a del Peru el año 1713," ARSI, Perú, 21, ff. 175–179v.
33 Livi Bacci, *Conquest*, p. 211.
34 Altamirano, *Historia*, p. 135.
35 "Carta del Padre Antonio de Orellana," in Maurtua, ed., *Juicio de límites*, vol. X. p. 23.

36 "Informe presentado al Rey por el Gobernador de Santa Cruz de la Sierra, Don Manuel Antonio de Argamoza, sobre el estado de las Misiones de Mojos y Chiquitos, en 1737," in M. Ballivián, ed., *Documentos para la Historia Geográfica de la República de Bolivia*. I: *Las Provincias de Mojos y Chiquitos*, La Paz: Gamarra, 1906.

37 D'Orbigny, *Descripción geográfica*, p. 352.

38 "Diego Ignacio Fernández al Padre General Miguel Ángel Tamburini," ARSI, Perú, 21, f. 126v. This letter was written on 21 September, 1711. Imagining a population of 30,000 and that deaths to children "before the age of reason" refer to children below the age of ten, and using the mortality of 1828–30 (48 per thousand) we would get about 1,440 deaths in all; the "nearly one thousand children" then would account for about two-thirds of the total. That proportion is compatible with a stable population having a very low life expectancy at birth of about 20 and an annual rate of growth of 1 percent (or alternatively a life expectancy of 22.5 and a rate of growth of 1.5 percent or again 25 years and 2 percent).

39 The *planillas* were a sort of "*Status animarum*" or a count of the inhabitants that the Fathers kept for each mission. They refer to the year's end and offer different levels of detail. The *planillas* for the thirty missions of Paraguay normally include a summary of baptisms, weddings, and burials (the latter distinguishing between children and adults in some cases). And while the statistical prospects in Paraguay reach a notable level of precision and detail, such was not the case for the Llanos. Few are known, and others still need to be brought to light in American and European archives. In this regard, see Barnadas's introduction to Eder, *Breve descripción*; Block's work *In Search of El Dorado*; and that of Tormo Sanz, *Historia demográfica*.

40 Non-baptized Indios, or *catecumenos*, already gathered in the missions numbered 4,955 (37 percent of the total population) in 1691, 6,555 (19 percent) in 1720, 3,771 (11 percent) in 1736, 1,213 (4 percent) in 1749 and 757 (2 percent) in 1752. See Block, *In Search of El Dorado*, p. 298.

41 These calculations are approximate at best. In any case, the 1831 count of the Llanos yielded 5,708 female *casadas* over the age of twelve. Average births for 1829–42 were 1,505 and overall fertility 65.8 per thousand. Assuming that 20 percent of the married women over twelve were over fifty (and so no longer fertile; this estimate is based on a stationary population with a life expectancy at birth of twenty-five) and subtracting the widows, the married women between twelve and fifty would number 4,566 and the legitimate fertility rate would equal 1,505 ÷ 4,566 × 1,000 = 330, a level close to the European average before the modern spread of birth control.

42 According to Eder, the Itonamas had very high fertility: "The Itonamas seemed to never tire of having children, so that it was truly impressive and amusing to see the multitude of children attending the usual lessons in catechism and the religious ceremonies" (Eder, *Breve descripción*, p. 341). Nonetheless, data from Santa María Magdalena, the mission founded in 1720 with Itonama converts, do not reveal structural particularities that suggest above average fertility.

43 See note 40.

44 Pastells, *Historia*, vol. VII (1948), p. 343.

45 Ibid., vol. VIII, t. I (1949), p. 656.

46 Ibid., p. 661.

47 Ibid., vol. VIII, t. II (1949), pp. XXIII–XXX.

48 Block, *In Search of El Dorado*, p. 327

49 Livi Bacci, *Conquest*, pp. 216–18.

50 Block, *In Search of El Dorado*, p. 338.

Epilog

1 The passage from the Portuguese traveler Manoel Felix is taken from Block, *In Search of El Dorado*, p. 232.

2 Eder, *Breve descripción*, p. 355.

3 Alcides Parejas, *Historia de Moxos y Chiquitos a fines del siglo XVIII*, La Paz: Instituto Boliviano de Cultura, 1976, p. 40.

4 Ibid.

5 Leandro Tormo Sanz, "El sistema comunalista indiano en la región comunera de Mojos Chiquitos," *Comunidades*, 1966, p. 40.

6 Ibid.

7 Parejas, *Historia de Moxos*, p. 39.

8 Tormo Sanz, "El sistema comunalista," p. 37

9 Moreno, *Catálogo*, p. 16.

10 Ibid.

11 D'Orbigny, *Descripción geográfica*, pp. 36–9; see also table A.3.

12 Ibid., p. 236; Moreno, *Catálogo*, pp. 106–7.

13 Moreno, *Catálogo*, p. 100.

14 Block, *In Search of El Dorado*, p. 332.

15 Moreno, *Catálogo*, p. 324; see also pp. 92–3, 325–8.

16 Ibid., p. 113.

17 Ibid., p. 335.

18 D'Orbigny, *Descripción geográfica*, p. 237. During the war for independence between 1810 and 1824, the region was left abandoned. In 1820 at San Pedro, Governor Velasco killed the *cacique* Marassa for insubordination, inciting the anger of the Indios who besieged the governor and his barricaded garrison, driving them out with fire and killing them. The revolt was put down by troops sent from Santa Cruz. The missions' archive was destroyed in the fire, and the capital of the region was transferred from San Pedro to Trinidad.

19 Block, *In Search of El Dorado*, pp. 337–8, 340.
20 D'Orbigny, *Descripción geográfica*, pp. 242–3.
21 Moreno, *Catálogo*, p. 72. Moreno wrote during the late 1880s when the Mojos region was in crisis.
22 Hernando Sanabria Fernández, *En busca de Eldorado*, La Paz: Librería Editorial Juventud, 1980, p. 29.
23 The citation is taken from Ibid., p. 35.
24 Ibid., pp. 36–7.
25 Ibid., pp. 40–1. See also Jean Claude Roux, "De los límites a la frontera. O los malentendidos de la geopolítica amazónica," *Revista de Indias*, LXI, 2001, n. 223, pp. 325–31.
26 Edward Davis Mathews, *Up the Amazon and Madeira Rivers through Bolivia and Peru*, London: S. Low, Marston, Searle & Rivington, 1879, pp. 132–3.
27 Moreno, *Catálogo*, p. 75.

INDEX

Note: Page numbers in italics refer to a map. Page numbers followed by *fig* refer to a figure; those followed by *n* to a note; those followed by *tab* to a table. Page numbers followed by *q* indicate the author of an unattributed quote. Illustrations in Plate sections are shown by plate numbers which appear after the page numbers.